The SURVIVAL
of the SOUL

Hay House Titles of Related Interest

YOU CAN HEAL YOUR LIFE, the movie,
starring Louise L. Hay & Friends
(available as a 1-DVD program and an expanded 2-DVD set)
Watch the trailer at: www.LouiseHayMovie.com

THE SHIFT, the movie, starring Dr. Wayne W. Dyer
(available as a 1-DVD program and an expanded 2-DVD set)
Watch the trailer at: **www.DyerMovie.com**

∾

*THE CRYSTAL CHILDREN: A Guide to the Newest Generation
of Psychic and Sensitive Children,* by Doreen Virtue

THE INDIGO CHILDREN: The New Kids Have Arrived,
by Lee Carroll and Jan Tober

*MESSAGES FROM SPIRIT: The Extraordinary Power of Oracles,
Omens, and Signs,* by Colette Baron-Reid

*THE MOTHER OF INVENTION: The Legacy of Barbara Marx
Hubbard and the Future of YOU,* by Neale Donald Walsch

THE POWER OF YOUR SPIRIT: A Guide to Joyful Living,
by Sonia Choquette (available May 2011)

THE SPIRIT WHISPERER: Chronicles of a Medium,
by John Holland

*TEMPLES ON THE OTHER SIDE: How Wisdom from
"Beyond the Veil" Can Help You Right Now,* by Sylvia Browne

*THIS IS THE MOMENT!: How One Man's Yearlong Journey
Captured the Power of Extraordinary Gratitude,* by Walter Green

*VISIONS, TRIPS, AND CROWDED ROOMS:
Who and What You See Before You Die,* by David Kessler

All of the above are available at your local bookstore,
or may be ordered by visiting:

Hay House USA: **www.hayhouse.com**®
Hay House Australia: **www.hayhouse.com.au**
Hay House UK: **www.hayhouse.co.uk**
Hay House South Africa: **www.hayhouse.co.za**
Hay House India: **www.hayhouse.co.in**

The SURVIVAL
of the SOUL

Lisa Williams

HAY HOUSE, INC.
Carlsbad, California • New York City
London • Sydney • Johannesburg
Vancouver • Hong Kong • New Delhi

Published and distributed in the United States by: Hay House, Inc.: www.hayhouse.com • *Published and distributed in Australia by:* Hay House Australia Pty. Ltd.: www.hayhouse.com.au • *Published and distributed in the United Kingdom by:* Hay House UK, Ltd.: www.hayhouse.co.uk • *Published and distributed in the Republic of South Africa by:* Hay House SA (Pty), Ltd.: www.hayhouse.co.za • *Distributed in Canada by:* Raincoast: www.raincoast.com • *Published in India by:* Hay House Publishers India: www.hayhouse.co.in

Project editor: Shannon Littrell • *Design:* Nick C. Welch

Library of Congress Cataloging-in-Publication Data

Williams, Lisa.
The survival of the soul / Lisa Williams. -- 1st ed.
p. cm.
ISBN 978-1-4019-2804-9 (hardcover : alk. paper) 1. Spiritualism. I. Title.
BF1261.2.W54 2011
202'.2--dc22
2010041896

Hardcover ISBN: 978-1-4019-2804-9
Digital ISBN: 978-1-4019-3086-8

14 13 12 11   4 3 2 1
1st edition, April 2011

Printed in the United States of America

*To my son, Charlie—
my inspiration, who has always
shown me the light with a smile
on his face and with love in his heart!*

CONTENTS

INTRODUCTION

The Survival of the Soul has arrived at a time when so many people are seeking to understand what happens when we leave this earthly life. *What happens when we die?* is a question I am asked by many people—understandably, as I am a psychic medium who speaks to dead people.

Lately, I've been hearing that question more frequently, as participants in my workshops and live readings express their curiosity about the Afterlife more than their desire for messages from their loved ones. It is because of such increasing interest that I have written a response in the form of this book.

Saying that I have the answer to what must be life's greatest mystery may sound presumptuous, going beyond what an ordinary person could ever hope to know. But I don't see myself as someone special to be placed on a pedestal. I am not that. What I write about in *The Survival of the Soul* was either told to me by Spirit through my readings for other people or communicated through my many spirit guides—those beings whose presence is energetic and have been with me through my life's journey. (Please note that *Spirit* is a term I use to refer collectively to those souls who have passed into the Afterlife.) My direct experience is also of value: yes, I have "died," but I didn't complete the transition; instead, I had a near-death experience, and was sent back to do my work on Earth.

I am simply a vehicle for knowledge and information to come through and be shared with those who want to know. I am not the source; in fact, we *all* have the ability to be psychic. Yet not every psychic is a medium. It takes practice—just like building a muscle through repeated exercise—to strengthen our ability to contact Spirit. To that end, I have developed my gift of psychic mediumship over many years, giving readings to individuals and large audiences (and on television) at locations all over the world. But most of all, I've learned that I always have to believe in myself.

How I came to my unique profession is a story I recount in my first book, *Life Among the Dead.* As a child I frequently saw and spoke to spirits, but I learned to hide what I eventually called my "gift," because people around me thought I was strange and were frightened by my ability to see dead people. Although my maternal grandmother, Frances Glazebrook, also worked as a medium, I had little contact with her as a child. Even so, when I was a teenager she told me that I'd be onstage in front of thousands of people doing what she called her "work."

When I did start to do readings professionally, I was shocked by how popular they were, but I never thought of becoming famous or going on TV. I was happy giving private readings daily and helping people on their journeys in life. Then about six years ago, I was working as a medium in the front room of my home in Redditch, England, when I was given an opportunity to go to Los Angeles for an extended period of time. This was made possible through a friend for whom I'd given a reading, and he encouraged me to take the time off and explore what L.A. was about. That trip changed my life.

They say there is no such thing as coincidence and that everything happens for a reason, so there was obviously a reason why I became terribly ill and had to be hospitalized during my stay in America. You see, for most of the three months that I was in Los Angeles, I fought a severe pelvic infection that didn't respond to the normal course of antibiotics. After surgery, the doctors felt it wasn't safe for me to fly back to England, so to recover, I extended my visa by an extra ten days.

During those ten days of recovery time, I gave a reading to a woman who asked me to meet a friend of hers named Merv Griffin. Apparently he was a "big deal" on TV in the States, but since I'm English, I had no idea who he was. I met with Merv, and over the course of some time, we bonded. I returned to America to work with him, creating a TV pilot that became *Lisa Williams: Life Among the Dead.* Thanks to the success of that show, my career has taken me all over the world, where I've taught psychic and mediumship development to small groups; and where I've stood onstage before thousands of people giving readings to large audiences—just as my grandmother said I would!

The Creation of This Book

The story of how I wrote this, my second book, is an interesting one that reveals much about how I work. To say the least, it did not go the way I expected. In fact, soon after I'd written many chapters of the first draft, I shredded the entire manuscript, realizing that I needed a different approach to this topic than my structured first attempt. This followed a dictation by my spirit guides, which I did my best to capture, letting my fingers fly across my computer keyboard as fast as they could go.

It started when I was in Australia in April 2009, doing four shows in Sydney and Melbourne. The country had been recently devastated by bush fires that struck just outside of Melbourne, so I donated the proceeds from my shows to recovery efforts. I also extended my stay to take a trip to Uluru/Ayers Rock, a huge monolith that I'd heard was a spiritual high point in central Australia.

I was sitting outside on the balcony of my hotel room near this sacred site, when I felt a sudden urgency to write. The idea came to me to write a book about what happens when we die. I started to use material I'd been given from readings I did as a medium—and then, almost immediately, I felt the presence of someone sitting by my side. I had no idea who it was, but I was aware of being fed information, as if in a dictation.

Okay, I thought, *I'll stop writing in a structured way and just take down everything I'm being given.* But first I asked, *Who are you?* and heard the reply: *I am Ariel.* At that point, the spirit Ariel gave me the material I typed as a transcript, which comprised a huge amount of information that I went on to use in this book.

A few months after my experience at Uluru/Ayers Rock, I was in New York after signing a publishing contract with Hay House. I'd just been on a cruise and was scheduled to go on tour, so instead of going back to the West Coast for what would have only been 36 hours, I decided to stay on for a few days in New York City and get started on the book.

You might not think that New York would be the right place to channel creative energies, but I found that it was . . . in fact, I ended up not leaving my room for a full three days. Thank goodness for room service, which allowed me to stay put and practice my yoga and still my mind, so I could become receptive for further input from Spirit.

After a while, I felt a presence behind me. I discovered that it was Ben, my spirit guide who has been with me for many years. He said, *I want to introduce you to someone, a spirit whose name is Josiah.* Ben then showed me a vision of myself writing in Australia, receiving information from Ariel. From that vision, I concluded that Josiah wanted me to receive and write material that he'd be giving me as well.

Once again I was led away from the formal structure of writing the book, as I'd already started organizing chapters after the channeling from Ariel. Now I sat still and thought, *Okay, I'm ready.*

Whenever I do a reading, I always start with an opening prayer, asking my spirit guides to give me the protection I need in order to correctly deliver the information I receive. I ask that the information come through clearly, accurately, and concisely, and I request only the most positive information. Then I close my eyes and feel an incoming energy merge with my own. In the hotel room that day, I received a very different energy from what I was used to—this energy I now felt was highly powerful, as if I were being connected directly to the Source of the universe.

I let my fingers be guided across the computer's keys. Through a tiny window in my hotel room, I could see trees and sky in the distance. I wasn't actually present in my body, but had floated out of it and sat with my guides for some time. It was only my physical body that did the typing, as my soul had come *out* of my body.

Since I wasn't present in my body, I had no idea what the conversation I was having with Spirit was about—and then suddenly, I got shoved back into it. My first thought was: *I need the loo.* I asked Ben, who was standing by, if I could go, and he said yes.

I need to look at what I've written, I thought, as I headed for the bathroom. My brain hadn't processed any of the information as it had come through, so I walked along with my laptop open, reading the words I'd typed. I was so fascinated by what I read that I never put the computer down, finishing in the bathroom and washing up while still reading it. I was absolutely gobsmacked by what I'd seen on that computer screen.

This is incredible! I thought. *I need to share it with someone.* Then I heard, *You have 20 minutes before we go again.* I took my laptop back to the desk and e-mailed a chunk of what I'd typed to my assistant, Caroline, and also to my friend Jonesy. Both of them responded immediately, saying, *Oh my God! Wow! It is truly incredible!*

The 20 minutes up, I felt a tapping in my head. *Okay, okay, I'm coming,* I replied and prepared to get back to work.

No. Move.

Move? I asked.

Yes. Move to a different location.

I sat on the bed, and again, the same spirit, Josiah, streamed information as I typed for another two hours.

When Ben had introduced me to Josiah, he'd told me that Josiah was an Elder who worked directly with Source, and the information he was giving me needed to be represented in a correct manner. Then there came a point toward the end of our "session" when I became present in my body and started to process what was coming through, probably so I could verify and clarify what I was getting. *Okay, I've got questions,* I said. And for another half hour, I asked for clarity on things I didn't understand, all the while processing this new information.

Finally, I went down to the hotel's business center and printed out what I'd written, which produced a thick pile of paper. I went back to my room and scrapped the more structured chapters I'd previously written. It was clear to me my book had to be based on the information I had been given by Spirit, and not my own mind.

About This Book—and This Series

The Survival of the Soul is the first in a series of books I'm writing called *DO YOU WANT TO KNOW EVERYTHING?* I chose that title for the series because it's the first question I ask people who come to me seeking answers—it's my way of getting permission to pass on whatever Spirit is giving me. I also want people to take ownership of the information I'm going to give them, to take responsibility for receiving it. Sometimes a message may not be pretty, but I never filter it. I try to deliver any "bad news" with as much diplomacy and love as possible, but I do need to know that a person is willing to hear the truth.

Each book in the *DO YOU WANT TO KNOW EVERYTHING?* series will focus on different topics that people have asked me about, but the information and knowledge is ultimately from Spirit. A few of the subjects I will cover in the series include how, as a parent, you can empower your children to develop their psychic abilities; and how to find or work with your soul mate, also known as your *twin flame.*

For this first book, Part I prepares you for your exploration of the Afterlife. Here, I present a detailed account of my communications with spirits as a child growing up. You may resonate with my story, as so many children are inherently psychic and have had to isolate themselves and their awareness so as not to upset those around them. Then I take on the subject of belief. It's a natural progression to handle this subject early on in the process, since I know too well that many people deal with a fair amount of doubts and taboos about the Afterlife—whether as a product of their religious upbringing or as a result of academic and/or scientific knowledge that has been imparted in some way. I then delve into the human inclination to negatively anticipate death, and my understanding of that tendency through experiencing the passing of my grandmother.

In Part II, I tell the story of my own near-death experience and how I passed through the veil and into "the white light" to the waiting arms of my grandmother Frances (whom I call "Nan Frances"). I go on to explore the alternate path for souls who cross over after lives that have caused much harm to others (hell is presented as a state of mind rather than an actual location). I'll then share much about your "family" of guides and loved ones who may await you in the Afterlife to ensure that your journey is a powerfully healing experience. You'll discover how the journey to the Afterlife is one of learning and growth, but once souls pass, they return for a time to check up on loved ones, offering comfort and explanations if needed.

Part III is about the process all souls go through in healing from the life they have left behind. Each chapter covers a "room," or stage of the process—from the first stage in the Waiting Room, where newly arrived souls are checked in and receive their Life Contracts, to the final stage in the Guardianship Room, where souls receive guidance and counsel prior to choosing a path in the Afterlife.

Part IV describes how souls, while still in the Afterlife, have an opportunity to choose their parents by carefully observing possible candidates in the Screening Room. In preparation for their reincarnation, souls draw up a new Life Contract and determine exactly what events and conditions are needed for their further evolution.

Introducing My Team of Spirit Guides

Throughout the book, you will meet the spirit guides I work with and, at times, directly read their words as I have transcribed them. I've briefly discussed three of them already, but I'd like to give you a more detailed introduction now:

— **Ben**, my master guide, has been with me all my life, but I have only been aware of him since starting my work as a medium. I lived a past life with Ben in which he helped save my life. Following that, we made an agreement for him to help others through me and my mission of teaching spirituality.

Ben showed up on a Sunday night when I was 27 years old, accompanied by my deceased grandmother. As she introduced the tall, dark, handsome stranger to me, she said, "I have taken you so far . . . I cannot take you any further. This is now Ben's work." He has been present in my life ever since and has given me guidance and clarity during many personal situations in life. But Ben's main purpose is to aid me in connecting the souls of those who have departed to those still left on the Earth plane.

— **Ariel** is a higher vibrational spirit who first channeled through me in the sacred place of Uluru/Ayers Rock in Australia in early 2009. I was meditating and watching the sunset when Ariel came to visit, and she gave me some of the information that forms the basis of this book. I am grateful to her for imparting the knowledge to me that will help so many.

— **Josiah** is a spirit who has visited me many times over the years, yet I had never been able to connect as closely with him as I do with Ben until recently. Josiah is an Elder, a role that is the step between a spirit guide and God. Through deep channeling and meditation, Josiah showed himself to me and was able to talk me through the process of the transition of life. He showed me the pathway and the different stages of death, and he explained how we can grow from within our soul and also connect with our Higher Self.

Those are my three main spiritual guides, but I also have other guides whom I work with on a daily basis for various reasons and who help me when needed depending on various situations that occur. Everyone has a team of guides, headed up by a master guide, and Ben is mine. You may not be aware of your own spirit guides, but rest assured that they are there. Your master guide instructs other helpers or guides to come in and assist you through different situations in *your* life. For example, one of the guides who helps me deliver messages is Lucinda. She is often present and gives me information when I teach and give readings to large audiences.

The information I've received from my team of spirit guides has been eye-opening, and I have personally learned many things about myself during this process. I've included several passages from transcripts that I've typed, so you can see exactly how my guides gave me the information I've used. Note that whenever one of my guides—or anyone else from the spirit realm—communicates in this book, it is indicated by the use of italics. I have also included reports or transcripts from some of the readings I have done for others, as aided by my guides. (Names and identities have been changed for confidentiality purposes.)

So, do *you* want to know everything? If you do, you will find the answers to many of your questions in the pages of this book. If you're truly ready, let's get started on this exciting journey together!

PART I

ORIENTATION

Timing is everything.
There are no coincidences.

CHAPTER 1

DISCOVERY

What happens when we die?

This is a question I've been asked many times over the years in my work as a psychic medium. And I have answered it often, as I deliver messages to people from their loved ones who are speaking from beyond the Earth plane. These messages always reveal a startling realm of knowledge about the Afterlife, assuring us that the soul does indeed survive.

Yet even as I developed in my work as a psychic medium, there were still many questions I needed to have answered. In my search to understand life's fuller journey, I have made myself available to Spirit and received information from what I can only call a Higher Source. I discovered in my quest that we are all—in death just as in life—on a rich and rewarding voyage, the purpose of which is our continued learning and growth. The soul, I've learned, not only survives but evolves, and how that unfolds is the subject of this book.

Throughout life, we all wonder why we're here and what our purpose is, and few of us know the answers to such questions. There are only a handful of individuals in the world who know their life's true calling and destiny, yet there are many who constantly search for it. They miss an important truth, though, which is that *the answers lie within.*

The answers I offer in *The Survival of the Soul* have all come from within, the deepest source of wisdom available to any human being. Throughout, I've drawn on evidence from the many readings I've given; the channeled messages I've received from my spirit guides; and my own personal experiences, such as a near-death experience (NDE) I had some years ago (and tell about in more detail in this book). Since childhood, I have connected deeply and often with Spirit, so this has always been a normal way of life for me.

My aim in this book is to answer your own questions about what happens when we die, helping you fully understand the journey we all must take and the lessons we must learn. Do you meet your family members who passed before you? Do you return back to the Earth plane after a time in the Afterlife? And most of all . . . is there *really* a God?

These are just some of the questions I will address in this book. But of one thing I am certain: Life is a journey for us all that never stops, not even after death. In fact, our departure from the physical world is the beginning of our rebirth into an eternal and everlasting life where we continue to love, learn, and grow. This is something I knew from my experience as a child, but came to doubt before embracing my full abilities as a psychic medium.

My Two Worlds

As adults, we usually don't remember the time spent in the Afterlife between our earthly lives (although some children do, for reasons I will explain in a later chapter). When *I* was a child, however, I had many memories as well as real experiences of the spirit realm—despite the fact that at times I thought I might be crazy!

It wasn't until I was older that my connection to Spirit was confirmed by a numerologist, who remarked, "You don't just communicate with the spirit realm—you *remember* it." Another confirmation came from an astrologer I consulted, who told me, "It's in your nature to be fascinated by death." I thought this was an odd comment, until she went on to say that I was using my fascination with death to help others, which was a completely accurate insight. It was a great relief to finally meet some people who understood me!

When I was younger, I didn't have such support for my experiences, some of which were disturbing to me when they occurred. Today I may be known as Lisa Williams, the psychic medium with her own TV shows who communicates with loved ones who have passed over. But when I was just a child—a child who saw dead people—I was afraid of seeing such spirits.

To be accurate, it wasn't the appearance of spirits that frightened me; nothing about their frequent comings and goings throughout my childhood seemed abnormal. I grew to fear their visits because of the reactions displayed by the adults around me. I was brought up in a Christian environment at school, and my father was (and still is) very much an atheist. When I told my family that I saw and spoke with spirits, I was quickly branded as having an "overactive imagination," which was the only way they could deal with what they saw as my worrisome behavior.

I learned to keep quiet about what was normal to me. Consequently, I was a rather isolated child, struggling to live in two very different worlds. In one, which included family and friends, I conformed to other people's ideas of life—going through the motions and listening to their opinions—and never mentioned my own reality. In the other, which was more real to me in many ways, my spirit friends and visitors talked to me. Throughout my childhood, I felt very much a part of my own world and quite detached from the one that others thought was real.

Yes, I saw the spirits of people who had crossed over; I spoke to them, and they spoke to me. But it was like talking to someone who was alive—and in my mind, they *were* alive. I could never understand the word *dead,* which carried a bewildering sense of finality when spoken by others. Being dead was something that did not exist in my reality.

My earliest memory of being spoken to by a spirit occurred when I was about three years old. I liked to play in my bedroom with my friends (the ones only I could see), a little boy and girl who had died in a fire and who used to visit me frequently. I would often notice a man in the room who sat and watched over us. Since he never said a word, I chose to ignore him. Meanwhile, my mom would be going about her day, taking care of my younger brother, Christian, and barely taking notice of the giggling coming from my bedroom—and if she did notice it, I'm sure she thought it was only "Lisa playing."

One evening I was called to dinner. The man who had been in my bedroom walked with me to the dining room—or rather, *floated* with me, as I never saw his legs—and sat down on a chair in the corner. I was seated at the table in front of my plate, which had some vegetables on it. As I was scooping up my peas on my fork to put in my mouth, something unexpected happened. The man spoke for the first time.

"Don't eat your peas or you'll die!" he warned.

Startled, I put my fork down and proceeded to eat all around the peas, careful not to put any in my mouth. My mother, of course, wanted to know why I wasn't eating my peas.

"He told me I would die if I did!" I told her, while pointing to the man in the corner of the room.

"Don't be silly—there's no one there," my mom replied, and then tried to persuade me to eat the peas.

But I refused and sat there stubbornly with my arms crossed and my mouth shut tight. Nothing was getting in my mouth, and not even a promise of ice cream for dessert would make me eat those little round green things that could kill me. *Never!*

I recall it was at that moment that my parents first declared I had an overactive imagination. But even today, I have an aversion to peas, in spite of what I recently discovered: that my father's great-uncle died while choking on a mouthful of peas! It must have been that great-uncle who watched over me as I played in my room and who tried to warn me about the "deadly" vegetable.

Nighttime Adventures

As long as my spirit visitors came during the day, I could play with them and have fun. But at night, it was a different matter. I had all sorts of people—not just children—popping in and out of my room when I was supposed to be sleeping. This so frightened me that I *couldn't* sleep. I hid under the covers to avoid these interlopers, but eventually I couldn't breathe and was forced out from hiding, often to find a woman standing at the foot of my bed with her hands on her hips looking angrily down at me. Back I went under the covers again. Coming up for air, I squeezed my eyes tightly shut so that I wouldn't see the spirits gathering in my room. But that didn't stop them from pulling my hair, poking at me, and talking to me. I buried my head under the pillow and hoped with all my might that they would go away. But they didn't.

I had other nocturnal experiences that were similarly unsettling. I remember being in bed and floating away from my body, looking back to see myself sleeping peacefully as I was flying above it. It was exhilarating at first. *Wow . . . I can fly!* I thought with a thrill, and off I went around the house to watch my brother sleeping or my mom and dad in the living room watching TV.

But then one night I found myself outside in the dark alone, some distance away from home. I was only four years old, and I knew right away that I shouldn't have left by myself. My mom had told me never to go outside after dark, because "bad people" were out there. Now I was outside and frightened, and didn't know what to do.

Looking around, I recognized the road I was on, but I didn't know how to get back to my house. I also recognized the place where my dad went to hit golf balls down the hill, so I knew I wasn't too far from home. But panic was setting in, and I started to cry—although the tears didn't roll down my cheeks as they would have had I been in my physical body.

I tried to shout, but no sound came out. I tried to talk to a man who was walking up the hill, but he ignored me as if I weren't there. Then I realized that I was flying and didn't have a mouth, much less a body. At that point, I saw the fellow who had told me not to eat my peas. Unlike the first man I'd seen, he could tell I was upset and offered to help me.

"Imagine yourself lying back in your bed all safe," he said.

So I did. I imagined myself surrounded by my stuffed animals, and I felt the warmth of the covers. Suddenly, I was swooshing back, pulled toward my bed by a force that seemed to come from

my tummy area. The strength of the pull had me whizzing past the streetlamps, up the stairs to the flat, through the door, past my mom and dad watching TV, and . . . *plop!* I was back in my bed.

I woke up crying, and I headed out to the living room to seek comfort from my parents after what had been a traumatic experience. But once comforted, I was still afraid to go back to bed and refused to budge from the living room. My parents could handle one night of this behavior—but when it became a nightly routine, they grew irritated and didn't know how to cope with the new situation.

One story that's been told and retold at family gatherings is how I refused to go to bed one night, and my dad switched the lights off and walked out of the living room, leaving me sitting there. Defiant and stubborn (and I haven't changed!), I didn't say a word, but just sat and stared at the door. Finally, guilt got the better of Dad—he came back into the living room, picked me up, and took me to my bed.

That was the start of a series of many such nights. One parent would say to the other, "It's your turn tonight," and I'd end up in my bed with either Mom or Dad squished up by my side with one arm wrapped around me for comfort. As a mother myself now, I understand the strain that I must have put on my parents' relationship; but at the time, I was so grateful to have someone there with me that I never thought of how it was for them.

Back then I didn't know that my nighttime excursions were instances of *astral-traveling,* a phenomenon in which the soul and body are separated while a person is still in earthly existence. Once separated, the soul is free to travel unhindered by the material plane, an experience that seems like flying. We all travel when we're asleep, but most of us usually aren't aware of it when—or even after—it happens.

As a child, I grew so frightened of traveling in this way that I'd automatically give myself a jolt to stop from going "out" when falling asleep, which could be a very unsettling feeling. Maybe you can recall having done this yourself: As you were falling asleep, your subconscious mind took over and your attachment to the physical plane weakened. At the same time, your vibration increased, making it easier for you to connect with the spirit realm. The memory of this occurring is rarely retained, but if you pay attention from this point on, you may notice it happening as you fall asleep.

The full memory of my childhood astral travels only became available to me during my deep meditations in adulthood. Now I realize that the funny feeling I had in my tummy when swooshing back into my body was my awareness of something called the *silver cord.* This is a link connecting the soul to our body as long as we're alive, and it's located an inch or so below the breastbone. The cord doesn't break until it's our time to cross over to the Afterlife. I think of it as the life force we all have, which comes from Source and keeps us plugged into our earthly existence.

Today I understand that while we're still on the Earth plane, the soul leaves the body often; this way, our body can receive healing if needed, or we can be educated subconsciously with information to help us along our path in life. Have you ever woken up after a night's sleep with the sense of knowing the answer to a question that troubled you before you fell asleep? Chances are that while you were out astral-traveling, information was being downloaded by Spirit to provide you with what you needed in order to resolve your dilemma.

Accepting My Gift

Growing up, I often felt like a bit of a loner. I had friends, but I was never "Miss Popularity." Yet one friend in particular, Samantha, helped me come to terms with what she first called my "gift." I was still very young when she used this word, and even though it felt strange to think that I had a gift, it also felt very right. I had no idea why she attributed this specialness to me at the time, since I never thought of myself as out of the ordinary. But after I'd demonstrated to her what she seemed to think were psychic abilities—knowing that a phone call would come from a particular person, for instance, or that another child would be absent from school before we got there—Sam was convinced I was "different."

Sam was the only person I had ever shared this information with, and slowly I started to accept that I did have something special that others didn't have. But I didn't take it very seriously. Between us, Sam and I would have fun with this gift of mine, laughing when a teacher confirmed something I already knew, such as that we were going to have a "surprise" quiz. It was amusing to play such games, and sharing my experiences with Sam was a big relief and helped me accept what I could do. Finally, a real person was part of my world!

∽

Life continued on, and so did my daily chats with Spirit. I tended to know when things would happen before they did, or I'd pick up on people's moods, even without them saying a word to me. It seemed that my gift had two gears: that of psychic intuition and that of communicating with the departed. It wasn't until I was 17 that I came to fully embrace my psychic abilities, though.

My friends and I had arranged a coach trip to Blackpool, a seaside town and resort in the north of England, which was just a good excuse to get away from school and have some fun. The outing included alcohol, but I refrained, never needing to drink to have a good time—although by looking at some of those old school pictures, you'd think I'd had a few! But that's just me expressing my silly side. What actually happened on that trip was profound and forever changed the way I looked at what Sam considered my gift.

Blackpool is home to three piers, each jutting out into the sea with different attractions for tourists to visit. One of them, known as the North Pier, was more refined and traditional than the other two. It didn't have as many facilities and amusement arcades as the others, so it appeared to give off an air of being a throwback in time, which made it an interesting place to visit. It was also quieter and more relaxed than its louder neighbors.

Strolling out on the North Pier, my friends and I noticed a sign in front of a tentlike structure that read: FORTUNE-TELLER. (I have never liked that term, but I accept that some people use it.) A few of us decided to have a reading "just for fun," but I didn't let on that I had several questions I very much wanted answered. I wanted to know more about a boy I liked, if I would pass the exams I was struggling with, and what I was going to do when I left school in a few months. You know, all the normal stuff that you think about when you're 17 and the world is your oyster.

One of the other girls went in before me, and after about 15 minutes, she emerged from the tent looking down and muttering, "Well, she's full of crap." Then it was my turn. I walked in through the draped entrance to a room that was quite tiny and hot. Two chairs were placed opposite each other, with a small table between them. On the table was a cloth, and on the cloth was a pack of tarot cards that, I remember recalling vaguely, resembled the deck of cards my Nan Frances—my grandmother on my mother's side—kept on the fireplace mantel in her house. It all looked very "witchy woo," a term I fondly use on occasion when referring to my psychic abilities.

The woman motioned for me to sit down without even looking at me. She had straggly blonde hair that hung below her shoulders, long pink nails that looked lethal, and layers of heavy makeup. She was dressed in a purple gown and wore dangling earrings, the typical palm-reader or fortune-teller costume I'd expected. Yes, she looked every bit the part.

Slowly, she looked up at me with her large blue eyes and, at the same time, swiftly grabbed the cards off the table. Once our eyes met, she placed the cards down in front of me and stared piercingly at me. I felt as if she were looking straight through me, and I felt so uncomfortable that I turned to see what was behind me.

"Interesting, very interesting," she remarked. Handing me the cards, she asked me to shuffle and cut them with my left hand and place them into three piles. By now I was nervous, but since I didn't want to upset her, I did exactly as she asked. Then she told me to pick two sets of cards.

Well, I thought, *which is the right one? How will I know if I've picked the right set?* But before I could finish the question in my mind, the woman said, "You will be drawn to the sets of cards that you need to work with. Do not choose; rather, let the cards jump out at you."

Wow, she heard me! So I did just that. Today I know that many people do the same thing when they face the prospect of selecting cards for a reading—they worry that they'll pick the wrong deck or set of cards. But as I was to find out, it's an opportunity to go with your gut instincts and give up wanting to control the outcome.

The woman moved around the cards that I'd chosen and then stared at me, which again made me uncomfortable.

"Is something wrong?" I asked, having no idea what she might be seeing—and, of course, I was thinking the worst.

She leaned in toward me and spoke very softly, as if she didn't want anyone else to hear what she was saying. "You have a gift," she said slowly. "But you don't know what to do about it." I sat there openmouthed, not knowing how to respond. "You are extremely powerful with your gift, so much more than I am," she continued. "I haven't seen this in a person for many years."

Well, that was it. It was now confirmed that what my friend had said when she walked out of the tent was true—this woman was truly full of crap. How could she tell a 17-year-old schoolgirl that she was more powerful than herself, the one giving the reading? It must be some kind of ruse. . . .

But wait a minute—how did she know about my gift? The thought kept me rooted to my chair. Then she let me ask her questions, and naturally I first wanted to know about boys. (She was right when she told me that the men in my life would never be the "right" ones.) I also wanted to know what type of job I'd have in the future. She said that I'd train for one vocational path, and while I'd go on to have many careers, only one would be meaningful. She told me that it would be a decision I'd have to make. Little did I know at that time that the decision I'd be making was about using my gift and making it my full-time profession.

I have always remembered the woman's parting words as I headed through the draped curtains of the tent toward my friends: "You will help many people and change their lives. Do not give up in this pursuit!"

Today I realize that this woman was an incredibly gifted psychic, one that others might have easily pooh-poohed because of her gimmicky appearance or because they weren't told what they wanted to hear. Looking back, I now realize that my friend who went into the tent first and came out muttering was possibly reacting to not getting the information that she thought she should have, and what the psychic had told her was probably spot-on!

As soon as I emerged, my friends gathered around me and wanted to know what the woman had told me. I made something up in reply because I wasn't ready to face the reality of the message I'd been given, even though my gift was normal to me (and still is). Somehow, the fortune-teller's acknowledgment of my gift and how I would help many individuals was too much for me to accept, and I wasn't sure I wanted the whole world to know about it. Now I see people react similarly to readings I give when the information coming through is too far afield from their current concept of themselves. But back then, I had no idea what the psychic was talking about, and even though her message made a profound impression on me, I kept it to myself.

My Grandmother's Influence

It was after this incident at Blackpool that I became curious about my maternal grandmother, Nan Frances. I knew that she worked as a psychic medium, giving readings out of her home, but I hadn't connected what she did with the Blackpool psychic—until I saw that they both used the same tarot cards.

I knew that my grandmother frequently had people coming by to see her, waiting patiently at the foot of the stairs leading to her lounge for their readings. I remember overhearing them chatting in low voices about what might happen if a certain loved one came through. But that was my Nan's life, something she'd always done as far back as I could remember. I never thought much about it, even when she warned me sternly to never touch the cards she kept on her fireplace mantel.

Then I had an opportunity to see Nan in action. I had moved away from home to start a new life in Hertfordshire, which was more than 100 miles away. My friend Sue, who had also grown up in Redditch, and I were headed home for a visit when we decided to pop in and see my grandmother. Nan welcomed us warmly and then abruptly asked us to sit at the circular table in the corner of a room that overlooked her garden. Once we were all seated, Nan looked straight at Sue and said, "David is here for you." She paused and then continued to give my friend a reading.

Even though Sue and I were close, I didn't know much about her family life. I only knew that she had a sister and didn't really get along with her mother, which was one of the reasons she'd moved to Hertfordshire. Sue later revealed that David was her father, who had died only a few years before. I had no idea. That was the first time I saw what Nan Frances could do, and I was amazed to experience the high energy I felt throughout the experience.

A few weeks later, it was *my* turn to have a reading. I was visiting again, and out of the blue, Nan said, "Lisa, I have to read for you." Of course, I was intrigued and let her go ahead. She then said something that I didn't understand at the time, but would later: "If I see my own death, I'm going to stop."

We sat at the same table where Sue and I had sat a few weeks earlier; only this time, Nan made me shuffle the cards. I felt very confused—Sue hadn't done that, so why was I being asked to?

I now know that Nan was about to give me a psychic reading, and she wanted to back up any information she got with the tarot cards, a common practice in readings. Sue's reading hadn't been psychic in nature; rather, it served to deliver a direct message from her dad, using my grandmother as a "medium" (hence the term). Because Nan was working with a different type of energy, that of a visiting spirit, she hadn't needed to use tarot cards with Sue.

This illustrates the difference between how psychics and mediums work. In a psychic reading, the reader is able to see events and situations that will happen in the future, using intuition and tapping into inner knowledge. As I've already mentioned, we are all psychic and have access to this kind of knowledge. Some call it *women's intuition,* while others call it *inner knowledge,* but it's what happens when you're in tune with yourself and listening to your Higher Self.

A medium, on the other hand, is the "middleman" from one realm to the next. A medium is like a radio transmitter and the spirits are the DJs, using the medium to get their message across to the person having the reading. The medium must finely tune in, making sure to connect to the right station, so the message can be heard as clearly and accurately as possible. All mediums tend to be psychic, but psychics are rarely mediums. Mediums don't use tarot cards but do employ other tools—such as holding on to personal items belonging to the client's loved one, or holding on to the hand, or something else, of the client herself.

Back at Nan's house, my dear grandmother made me shuffle the cards and cut them into three piles. I didn't need to use a specific hand to cut them, as I did with the Blackpool psychic, which again confused me. Nan Frances then told me to choose a pile I did *not* want to look at and put it aside. Hearing that, some panic set in: *What if I choose the wrong pile? Am I giving away my future to a bad set of cards? Oh no . . . decisions, decisions.* I hated the feeling of uncertainty, but as the Blackpool psychic had advised me to do, I went with what I felt and trusted my instincts (even though I was so intrigued that I wanted to see *all* the cards).

Next I was asked to choose a pile to work with first and then a pile to work with second. This was an easier task, as I knew I was going to look at both of them. (Silly, really—I suppose I'm just nosy!)

I asked Nan why she didn't want to look at the third pile that had been set aside. "That's your past, and you can't change your past," she replied. "The other two piles are your present and your future. It is there that we will focus."

So I can change the events that are in the cards? I wondered.

She must have heard my thoughts, because she said, "No, you can't change predestined events. Those events have been already decided to teach you lessons in life, but you do have free will. Free will gives you the ability to choose to learn your lessons or not. However, if certain situations are meant to happen, they will."

The reading began. I instantly thought about the guy I was dating—was he "the one"? And the job I had at the time—was it going to change? Would I ever become a singer and have a professional career? Looking back, my concerns and questions were shallow and selfish, but they were important to me then. I needed answers.

When it seemed that the reading was winding down, Nan looked at me and then above me, just as the Blackpool psychic had done before. *What is it with psychics looking at me and then around me?* I wondered. Then she spoke.

"You have the purple and yellow light above your head."

I looked up to see what she was talking about. *What light?* I couldn't see anything. But she continued, saying that she knew I wanted to know answers to certain questions, and she quickly answered the main ones. No, I wasn't with Mr. Right. And yes, the job was going to change.

The mundane stuff over, it was time for her to tell me the things I *didn't* want to hear. But before she did, she gave a gentle warning: this was information I had to be told and needed to listen carefully to.

The first thing she said was that I would be famous. Now, when we're younger, we all want to hear that we'll have fame because of the glitz and glamour that magazines and movies portray. I just wanted to sing, though—I hoped the fame she was talking about referred to an upcoming record contract. But how far from the truth I was! Nan said that I would be known for the work I did, and that it was the same work *she* did. I would continue with her work, but I'd be standing onstage, acting as a medium in front of thousands of people all over the world.

At the time, I was so stunned to hear that this was my future that you could have knocked me over with a feather. But today I can't imagine doing anything else. Thankfully, my shallowness vanished soon after that first reading, due to the many life-altering events I was to experience, such as having cancer and becoming a single mother. (I tell of these, and many other, experiences that shaped my path and led me to be able to do my work in my first book, *Life Among the Dead*.)

Today, I am in "the industry," as working in Hollywood is referred to, but it's still *not* about the glitz and the glamour for me. The work I do—as had been predicted—is helping people heal, while coming to terms with their journeys through life *and* death.

Starting to Work

It was only after my grandmother passed away that I finally began to work as a professional medium. Nan had never given me any training for developing my gift, however, so I was on my own when it came to setting up readings for people. Fortunately, a friend with more business sense than I suggested that I do a reading for her and charge 20 pounds, which is approximately 35 dollars.

One thing my grandmother said that has stayed with me through the years is: "Always trust your gut instinct—it will never let you down." The Blackpool psychic of my schoolgirl days had given me the same message, and it remains a powerful mantra that I share with my students who are trying to develop their own psychic abilities.

As I grew into my adult years, I finally accepted that being a psychic and a medium is part of who I am. I could never change or hide from it. Slowly, I started to embrace it, but my path wasn't easy. I had the support of friends (and, less so, my family), who urged me to finally come out and do readings as a full-time medium—and to announce to the world that this is who I am and what I do.

As soon as I started working professionally, I found that more and more people were accepting of what I did. Mediumship no longer had a stigma attached to it. It wasn't something that needed to be kept hidden away in heavily draped tents and behind closed doors. You didn't have to be a certain type of person who dressed a certain way to practice this gift, and you didn't even have to be shy about it.

Looking back, this new awareness was quite liberating—to know that I didn't have to be what people might have expected when they walked in my door for a reading. I was younger, kind of funky and fun, and I looked entirely normal. Furthermore, I incorporated my psychic skills into my everyday life. Since I was the mother of a young child, for instance, people knew me as someone who had all the concerns a mother has. My life and my work were not artificially divided between normal and "witchy," as had been the case in the past when mediums needed to have a "cover." I enjoyed a new kind of integrity, as hiding who I was had become totally unnecessary.

Another discovery I made as I gave more and more readings was that the more I worked with my gift, the stronger it became. In the same way that the more a singer sings, the wider her vocal range becomes, the more readings I did, the clearer the information was and the more it flowed. I was giving psychic readings initially, but then they evolved into mediumship readings. I was, and still am, very happy to do both.

I learned that there were different energies I could work with, depending on whether a reading is a psychic reading or a message from the Afterlife. I liken the two approaches to ascending two different staircases: I go up the psychic staircase to open myself up to a person's destiny and pathway; alternatively, I go up the mediumship staircase when I open myself up to the spirit realm. It always takes more energy to go up the mediumship staircase, but it's well worth it because it really helps people communicate with loved ones who have passed. I'm not saying that psychic readings are unable to help others, as they can provide so much clarity and hope in certain situations, but the mediumship route to me is more rewarding.

Sometimes I find that I need to switch staircases midway to check information given through one approach or the other. There have been times when I started up the mediumship staircase, receiving information from Spirit, and then had to switch to check on the accuracy—a kind of spirit-realm cross-referencing and back-up procedure. This is always a challenge to do, but it's also fun, especially when it yields confirmation.

This is exactly what happened on one occasion when a client named Claire came to see me. She wanted to connect with her grandmother, who had passed away while Claire was on holiday, so they didn't have a chance to say good-bye. As I started Claire's reading, her grandmother immediately came through and validated her presence by giving my client some personal information that only she knew. It was a beautiful connection and very powerful.

Then the grandmother started to tell Claire some things about her private life. She told her granddaughter that the man Claire was dating wasn't the right one for her and that she would wake up one morning, look at him, and simply say, "I don't love you anymore. We need to split up." There would be some loose ends to clean up, but Claire and her boyfriend would eventually part, leaving my client much happier.

After her grandmother started to close the connection down and the reading was coming to an end, Claire expressed to me that she felt a bit overwhelmed by the message, saying that it wasn't in her nature to break off a relationship in the way her grandmother predicted would occur. Due to her comment, I decided to look further into the reading about her life and check the facts by taking the psychic-reading approach. I asked for my spirit guide to connect me with Claire's spirit guide and provide any additional information. The energy shifted, creating the lighter feeling that is often characteristic of a psychic reading, and then the information began to flow.

My guide showed me a vision of Claire packing up some cases and boxes, but it was clear they did not belong to her. It turns out that I was seeing the scene of Claire's boyfriend moving out after she told him to leave, and she was helping him pack his things. I could also see a time frame in which all of this would happen. This psychic vision was exactly how Claire's grandmother had said things would occur.

Eighteen months later, I was shopping in a local store when I bumped into Claire. She filled me in on what had transpired in her life after she'd had that reading with me. Things had turned out exactly how her grandmother and my spirit guide had predicted—Claire had asked her boyfriend to leave—and she was so much happier now, which her grandmother had also predicted.

My Gift Today

I've now been working as a medium for many years and had an almost daily communication with the Afterlife. Unlike when I was a child, however, it is my choice to open myself up and allow spirits to deliver messages to their loved ones who are still on the Earth plane. For those of you who need me to put it bluntly: *I speak to dead people!*

It's no different from what you've seen in the many movies and television programs about psychics and mediums—such as *Ghost Whisperer, Medium, The Sixth Sense,* and *Ghost,* to name a few—only I do the real thing. I communicate and pass on messages of love, comfort, hope, and healing from loved ones who have crossed over to the Afterlife.

My path has not been an easy one. Even today, there are still times when I question it, but it's a path I adore. I've had to learn many life lessons along the way, and I'm still learning—a process you'll understand better after you've read this book. As I continue to grow, Spirit always surprises me and makes it fun by throwing something unexpected my way. I never know what is going to come out. That's why, before any reading I do, I always ask the person: "Do you want to know everything?"

For me, being a psychic and a medium is the best job ever. I love having the chance to assist people in finding closure after losing a loved one, giving them the chance to say good-bye, helping solve a mystery or murder, or just helping two souls connect and be able to have a conversation. Often people ask me, "Do you see this ability as a gift or a curse?" and I have to laugh. To me, it's always a gift, one I can't imagine living without.

∽◦∽

CHAPTER 2

SKEPTICS AND CYNICS

Perhaps you've sought a reading from a medium or psychic before; on the other hand, maybe you've never had such an experience. Either way, you may be like many people and question the reality of contact with the spirit realm, wondering what value there could be in reading this book. To this, I say: Don't let your beliefs or opinions stop you from exploring growth and healing opportunities. An open mind can reap incredible rewards.

Varieties of Response

Everyone has a different reason for connecting with the After-life, and each person's response varies according to the message he or she receives. Most individuals take what they want from the communication, absorbing only what will help them at the present time. Then, at a later date, they may fully understand or remember the whole message and be able to use it for their healing and growth. Others fully embrace the information at the time they receive it and accept that it is coming through for a higher purpose.

There are still others who come to me for a reading and are not quite sure what to make of the message they receive. These are either skeptics or cynics, and they may be holding beliefs that make it difficult for them to accept what I do. In this chapter I address their responses, as I believe it is important to deal with the reality of people's reactions up front and let readers know my views on this matter.

∾

Skeptics and cynics distinguish themselves by asking some version of this question: "How do you know this?" Sometimes I'll read for a person whose only purpose in getting a reading is to see for him- or herself if what I'm doing is the real thing.

I recall one man in particular who looked puzzled when I said, "Your grandfather Arthur is here." He then asked me, the challenge clear in his tone, "How did you know my grandfather's name was Arthur?" Instead of accepting that his grandfather was actually there, ready to give him a message, this man questioned my source, suspecting that I'd gotten the information from someone other than his grandfather. He was more interested in interrogating me than in getting value from the reading.

While skeptics may have their doubts, they haven't completely made up their minds and remain open—unlike cynics, whose doubt is more firmly entrenched. Even if I chose to prove to cynics that my work is real, I wouldn't be able to change their minds. The ones I've encountered want absolute validation, such as full names, addresses, and telephone numbers, as if my coming up with that information makes the messages I have for them somehow "real." Then after I give them what they want, they try to prove that I looked up the information on the Internet before they'd arrived for the reading!

Fortunately, the majority of people who come to me for a reading are open-minded, including those with varying religious viewpoints (a subject I will focus on in the next chapter). Even if they are a bit disbelieving at the outset, I don't mind . . . as long as the information they receive somehow helps them on their journey through life. That is the main purpose of my readings: to help people grow and move on. The reality is that I am communicating with the Afterlife, and it's the knowledge I receive from the souls who contact me that I share, not my own views or agendas.

I feel that it's important to address this issue of doubt and belief now before you read any further, as there are many skeptics, cynics, and nonbelievers out there who will be the first to criticize this book or my abilities. I've had to deal with them all my life; in fact, I have actually lived with them.

But first, I want to explore how we form our opinions about the Afterlife and all things spiritual.

Childhood and Beliefs

We're all influenced by the opinions of those around us, starting from a very early age. As a mother, I want my son to grow up with his own opinions, but I know that my actions and the things I like and dislike are going to influence him now. It's impossible to prevent this.

When we were tiny children, we were all molded by our parents, guardians, and others who were in our sphere. They had strong beliefs and talked about them, often expressing much emotion; consequently, we learned what was "right" and "wrong." We believed that what these grown-ups said was so because they were there to look after us, and we had no reason *not* to believe them.

I remember listening to my father and grandfather argue about politics every Sunday afternoon, and I found that even though I wasn't listening directly to their heated debate about which was the right party to run the country, I still adopted their views. Then when I heard other people talking about politics, I found that I'd have an opinion based upon what I'd heard the week before from one of these family discussions.

When it comes to the subject of the Afterlife, adults often have very strong opinions, and this is where kids can become confused. Since young children have the purest of vibrations and haven't yet been tainted by the values of others, they're naturally open to the world of spirits and the Afterlife. They are yet to develop their own views and are still innocent and pure, finding their way in the world and possessing that wide-eyed wonder that adults no longer have.

Because their perception of things is so untainted, children often remember their past lives, as well as events that occurred in the Afterlife before they reincarnated once again. They may even remember their conversations with God and other discussions that took place before they were born. Little ones so often display knowledge and wisdom that is truly profound, leaving us to wonder where it came from. This is because children are so in tune with their souls, and the soul is what holds the knowledge that we all need to know.

Kids also look at situations in a very black-and-white way. They never see the gray areas, and that's because they don't judge. It's when we judge that we lay our opinions on others. For example, my son, Charlie, recently wanted to know why one of my friends was upset, so I told him the truth. I said that my friend was married to someone who made her very sad, and she didn't know what to do.

"Well, it's simple," Charlie responded. "She should leave him and find someone who makes her happy again." I told him it wasn't that easy, since my friend and her partner had children together, but this wasn't an obstacle to my son.

"Mommy, we live together, so her children can live with her," he replied, holding no judgments or concerns about financial complications or the upheaval of a family. To him, the solution had no gray areas, but was a simple case of black-and-white choices to be made. Some may think this is an irresponsible view for an adult to hold, but after my separation, the fact is that it came down to Charlie and me following the exact path my son had prescribed— in the end, all the other concerns weren't nearly as important as the happiness in our current lives.

Each child is delivered to us straight from Source, which resides in the Afterlife, the place we all originate from. His or her body may be new, but the soul that incarnates in that body is often very old. Kids have lived on this planet before and bring from the spirit world the knowledge that we need to help heal many situations, such as angry provocations, emotional upsets, and even physical abuse and fighting.

Everyone comes to the Earth plane with a purpose or lessons that need to be learned (and I will discuss this in subsequent chapters), but there are some children who come along with the beautiful gift of spirituality and healing. Books have been written about them of late, calling them the "Indigo" or "Crystal" children, denoting that they have special gifts to further the evolution of humans on our planet. Such souls have retained their knowledge from their time in the Afterlife within their consciousness, and they know what lessons they are here to learn. But even these kids are sometimes unable to communicate that knowledge, being too young to find the words to articulate it.

Because of their closeness to Source, all children's vibrations are higher than those of adults. You may have noticed that babies have a soft spot at the top of their skulls where the bones haven't fused together yet; it turns out that this opening leaves the crown chakra exposed. This is the chakra for intuition and spiritual knowledge, and it is also a direct link to the spirit realm. That's why many babies, toddlers, and small children can see and sense spirits. They may have imaginary friends as well; however, these friends tend to be souls that they knew in the Afterlife who are connecting with them now.

Mothers notice how their babies sometimes stare at a certain corner of a room, as if communicating with someone they cannot see. When the mother goes to the place her baby has been look-ing at, she may feel a coldness in the air, making her momentarily shiver. That is a sign that the baby was looking at a spirit, whose presence is signaled by the air suddenly going cold, almost like when a refrigerator door is opened.

Another way that children let us know of their connection to the Afterlife is by telling us that they have a different name than the one given to them by their parents. In the Afterlife, we all have a name that our soul is known by, so it is not unusual for a child to insist that he or she be called by that original soul name. For instance, when my son, Charlie, was between the ages of three and five, he would insist upon being called Sam. I had no idea why he was telling me this, but I understood—because as a child, *I'd* always wanted to be called Victoria.

One day when Charlie was in his characteristic, open-to-talking mood, I asked him why he wanted to be called Sam. "Mommy, that was my name in heaven," he replied. I was blown away! "Charlie feels strange to me," he continued, "and I want to be called Sam."

In the same conversation, I asked my little boy if he remembered anything else from heaven, and he said, "Yes, Mommy. God told me I had to come and look after you, since Daddy didn't love you and you needed more love." Again, I was blown away, realizing from his words that it had been predestined for me to be a single mom and have relationship issues with men . . . but that is another book entirely!

I couldn't argue with my son's choice of names, so for two years I went along as he kept his other name, signing his Mother's Day and birthday cards to me with "Love, Sam." Eventually, he went back to using the name given to him in this life, Charlie, probably because he'd gotten used to it as he grew older.

૭∕ე

Children can become terribly confused about spirituality if the adults around them do not respond in any validating way. Boys and girls frequently struggle with what they know and believe, particularly when it conflicts with what their parents, guardians, or other authority figures tell them. Often kids are not heard when they speak from their innate spiritual knowing—which is exactly what happened to me when I was young, so I understand the torment that can happen internally.

No matter what your opinions may be on this subject, it is so important to be respectful of children expressing their beliefs. Remember, kids are closer to Source than we adults are, so their thoughts and experiences are seriously worth listening to. Keep in mind that they may block their senses to cut themselves off from any contact with Spirit, though, because they fear a negative reaction and don't want to upset the adults around them. It may take them a while to speak about their experiences, so it's vital to keep the lines of communication open and listen to what they say without doubting or categorizing them.

As we human beings get older, our opinions on many issues change, because society influences us. On the other hand, some individuals remain open to Spirit in spite of society's influence— and if one does remain open past the age of eight, then there is a good chance that he or she will grow up to be a very spirituality gifted person.

For example, my brother, Christian, used to hear and talk to spirits all the time when he was a child. He was extremely open and could have developed this gift further if he'd allowed himself to do so. However, he has actually become one the biggest skeptics I know.

The morning that our grandfather died, I found my brother outside of my grandparents' home extremely distraught. I calmed him down and asked him what was wrong, other than the obvious grief resulting from having lost a loved one. He replied, "I just heard him," in a scared and puzzled tone. "I just heard him," he repeated. "He spoke to me, and I'm freaking out."

I knew what Christian was talking about: Granddad had come along to say his last good-bye, which was totally his style. What surprised me was the way my brother reacted, so frightened by receiving this communication from our grandfather as he made his crossing over. I am not sure if my brother will ever be willing to accept that this actually happened, but it did.

The Cynics Among Us

In spite of the perspective we all have as children, many people are unable to accept the reality of communication with the Afterlife when they become adults. Sadly, they will readily shut the subject down, arguing against it until they're blue in the face. These men and women are not willing to see the endless possibilities the universe has to offer, making them life's cynics.

Cynics can be disbelievers about anything. I have encountered, and even read for, many of them in my experience as a psychic and medium. In some specific instances, I was left wondering why I even made the effort. These people were dead set against getting any value out of their readings, only wanting to confirm their own conclusion, which was that I couldn't possibly be the "real deal."

This happened once on national television. I'd been invited to appear on *The Oprah Winfrey Show* along with two other mediums,

John Edward and Allison DuBois, to discuss spirituality and to determine if people really could communicate with "the other side." We were each asked to read for three different people; during my final reading, I dealt with a woman who was clearly a nonbeliever.

Right before the taping of this reading, I turned to my makeup artist and my publicist and said, "The next person wants to get in touch with a father figure." These two close girlfriends had seen me work before and never doubted my abilities, so they simply responded, "Well, you should know!" They were right—I was correct. But I hadn't been prepared for what followed.

I walked into the studio for the taping and came face-to-face with Laura, a scientist and a cynic. I began reading for her, and the information coming through was clear and, in my mind, accurate.

I informed this woman that a father figure had shown up for her, and she responded, "Well, everyone has a father, so I guess I could relate to a father figure." At that point, I stopped to ask her outright if her father had passed. I explained that *my* father hadn't passed yet, so not everyone had a father figure in Spirit. She affirmed that yes, her father had died.

I continued, telling Laura that her father was saying the words *little girl*. "My father never called me his 'little girl,' even though I was the youngest of four," she snorted. "But, of course, in any father-daughter relationship, you could assume such an interaction. It would be a good guess."

Millions were watching this show, and at the risk of sounding too harsh, I point-blank asked her why she would want a reading if she wasn't going to accept any of the information I was giving her. At that point she turned to the producers of the show, who were sitting offstage, and asked in exasperation, "Am I being too skeptical?" Naturally, they didn't reply, but it was clear that Laura was sticking to her guns.

The reading continued. When I mentioned that her father was giving me the name "John," she quickly informed me that her father's name was not John. Rather, he was always called by his full name, which began with John but had an added name, like

John-Roger or John-Michael. It seemed that she was grasping at straws!

I went on to tell this woman that her father was showing me a vision of him dancing, and it seemed that he was dancing with *her.* She scowled and waved me off. "I never danced with my father. He was a ballroom dancer, but *I* never danced with him."

It was now clear that there was no way Laura the scientist was going to accept any information I was giving her—she had already determined that I wasn't talking to the spirit of her father.

I'm sad to say that people like Laura often miss out on huge opportunities to connect with family members whom they dearly loved. If they opened themselves up to a view other than a scientific, objective one, they could receive much value from a reading. But instead, they choose to fight the process, trying so hard to be right and prove me wrong!

༺༘

Over the years, I've come to learn that when people are cynical, I can never change their minds. They insist on some form of validation—such as cold, hard facts—in order to be convinced. But when spirits communicate from the Afterlife, they do so mostly through thought processes and visions, not through facts. They don't even have mouths to form the words, so what they say is muffled and very difficult to understand. I don't always catch all the words in a sentence either, so I can only present the information that I receive. This is great fuel for a cynic who is just waiting for unclear or incorrect information.

Sometimes the information coming through doesn't seem to make any sense at first, but if the client and I stay with it, the meaning becomes clear. For instance, I've had spirits give names that only I could relate to as a way to get information across. I remember reading for a woman who came to me because she had lost her son and wanted to communicate with him. I received her son's spirit, but the vision I was getting was the face of my ex-boyfriend Colin. I had no idea why he, of all people, had jumped into my brain.

In the reading, I clearly established that this woman's son had passed in a car accident and given her other identifying facts that only her son would know. Yet she still wanted more validation that it was really him.

"I can see my ex-boyfriend here, and I'm not sure why, but I'm going to describe him to you to see if you can relate it to your son," I told her. I then went through everything, telling her what Colin looked like, the car he drove, and the places he liked. But she couldn't relate to any of it.

Suddenly, her son's spirit nudged me and said the word *name*. "Oh, by the way, my ex-boyfriend's name was Colin," I blurted out.

Her face lit up like a Christmas tree. "*His* name was Colin!" she exclaimed, now happy and excited. Her son had used the reference of my ex-boyfriend to give me the important piece of information this woman needed in order to know he was really there. The point is that Spirit doesn't always come through in ways that are logical or factual at first, and to get value from any communication, it takes a willingness to suspend the usual requirements that everything "make sense."

Skepticism: A Healthy and Challenging View

While cynicism can be a huge problem because the person is virtually stuck in a position and cannot see beyond it, skepticism can be positive and healthy. In fact, I used to be (and still can be at times) a skeptic myself. I'm not skeptical about communication with Spirit being real, because I know it is—I wouldn't be true to myself and this book otherwise. But I am always skeptical at first about the gifts that people claim to have. I know that there are some individuals out there claiming to connect with the Afterlife who are only too ready to take hard-earned money from others. I have even been to some of these so-called mediums myself and, as I've sat for my reading, have wondered, *Why am I here, when this person obviously doesn't have the gift?*

When I think of skeptics, my father immediately comes to mind. It's hard to accept that he lived with me for almost 20 years and was married to someone whose mother was a well-known psychic even before that, but he still wouldn't believe in what we were doing. When I started to give readings, Dad would just shake his head and turn away. He never came to any of the shows that I put on in the U.K. or attended any of the spiritual church gatherings where I was the featured medium for the night.

Years after I'd started to give readings on a professional basis and was working as a full-time psychic medium, my father would still ask me, "When are you going to get a proper job?" My answer to that was, "What is a proper job?" And I left it like that; there was no point in arguing with him.

The first time he attended one of my public readings was in April 2008, and it was because he couldn't avoid it. We were on a ship in the middle of the ocean, on a cruise with the theme of spiritual connections that Hay House had sponsored. So unless Dad wanted to swim to land, he had to come and see my show.

I never get nervous before going onstage, but with my father in the audience, this time I was. I started my talk by asking if there were any skeptics in the room, and although many looked around, there were no raised hands. I waited and then pointed out my dad, saying, "I know we have at least one skeptic here, and that would be my father!" Everyone was shocked, and Dad just waved graciously, bless him.

The reason I pointed out my father wasn't because I wanted to embarrass him, but rather to show people that it's okay to be skeptical, to search for answers and question what you get. I explained to the audience that Dad's skepticism had been good for me as I was growing up. He'd challenged me when I was first developing my gift, which helped me realize that I had to work to convince other skeptical folks out there. It made me try harder to get *accurate* information, not just the general information that anyone could pick up. I worked hard to understand people, to empathize with them, and for this, I thank my father for his unshakable views.

Now I appreciate any skeptic who comes to a show or gets a reading, for I know that this person will challenge me to do my very best. When I meet those who tell me that they came to my show as skeptics and left as believers, I always ask at what point they changed their minds. They usually tell me that it was a reading they could relate to, or that I read for another person and they overheard him or her talking later about how spot-on it was. Often people will acknowledge the truth of a message more after the reading, and reveal how impressed they are with the answers they were given.

My father watched my TV programs and attended many of my live shows before he was convinced that what I did was in fact real. The week of the Hay House cruise, during which he attended every lecture I gave and even participated in some of the group exercises, it was still not enough to persuade him. He also went to many different workshops on spirituality that were given by others. He'd done his homework but still remained on the fence.

Then my grandmother, Dad's mother, passed in April 2009. On the afternoon after her funeral, we all returned to my parents' home to have some quiet time. My brother, Christian, and his wife, Claire, were in their room sleeping; Mom was resting in the living room; and Dad was in my parents' bedroom. Suddenly, he got up and called out, "Just a minute, Mom!"

My mother asked my father what was going on. He shook his head and said that he thought he'd heard his mother calling to him as he was drifting off to sleep, and her call woke him up. He then realized what he'd said and tried to take it back: "Oh, it must have been something I heard on the radio." My parents don't own a radio, and the TV was off—the house was perfectly quiet. So it seems as though Dad's mother had come to see him and had connected with him while he was dreaming, which is very common.

To be honest, my father's skepticism has never really bothered me. It wasn't until September 2009 that he finally came up to me after a show I did in Wellington, New Zealand, and said, "I believe you." Well, you could have knocked me over with a feather!

Dad had attended nine shows, watching how people in the audience reacted, and he'd make comments like: "That reading you did . . . the woman wasn't giving you anything, was she? But you did it. You brought her mother forward, and she was so happy in the end." So I knew I was making headway. Then when Dad finally made up his own mind about what I did, he embraced it.

Later, my father told me that he was actually afraid of my gift, because there was no logical explanation for it. "You're my daughter, and I know you don't lie," he said. "But I can't figure it out. I just know you give people hope and comfort, and that is a priceless gift. You've done your job."

Dealing with Skeptics—Myself Included!

Living with a skeptic when I was a child was hard for me, especially when I had gifts and abilities that I couldn't possibly understand. Having said that, I believe it's healthy for all of us to question what is real and what isn't, and I feel that we must make up our own minds about what to believe and what not to believe. This applies to me, too—even though I'm a professional medium, I maintain an air of skepticism when I receive a reading from another in my field.

Early on in my career, I once went to see a woman who told me what she thought I wanted to know about the future, rather than revealing anything that was actually useful. I felt cheated, as if I'd wasted my money, and the experience made me wary. Eventually, I got over it and visited another medium who was more helpful. She told me about my present life and also what had happened in the past, all accurate information that gave me faith in what she was saying. Then when she told me about the future, I received this message with an open mind.

Sometimes you know what is going to happen in life, as events are already mapped out and you can see the pathway. I'd had such a vision of my future at the time I sought the second medium, and I was amazed when she picked up on what I already knew.

My own vision was that I'd be onstage, communicating with a large audience of people. I loved music and also worked professionally as a singer, but I hadn't gone in that direction as a career. In my vision I wasn't singing, but I was still standing onstage, speaking to audiences, making people laugh, and even bringing them to tears. Still, I wasn't convinced that I would become a professional medium.

I also had another vision of my future at the time, in which I saw my name on the spine of a book that sat on a shelf. It was quite bizarre, as I'd never taken any interest in writing at school— although I had forced myself to study English at an advanced level, believing that somehow it would come in handy in life.

When I visited that second medium, she said I'd be onstage, but it wouldn't be in the way I might anticipate. Although everyone expected me to be singing at the time, this woman said that I'd be up there doing something totally different, and through my work, I'd also write books. Incredible, really, as this is what I'm doing right now!

This particular medium relayed other information that was correct over the course of time and completely restored my faith in psychics. As a result of that experience, I became less of a skeptic. Then when I gave my first reading—a story I tell in my first book, *Life Among the Dead*—I became even more convinced.

I did my first full reading spontaneously over the telephone while talking casually with a friend. She asked me what I thought about her boyfriend, and I told her the truth: he was cheating on her. I gave her a great deal of information, including the name of the woman he was seeing and where she worked. Over the next few weeks, I was totally gobsmacked when things I'd said unfolded as predicted. I was even less of a skeptic after that, and my faith continued to get stronger and stronger until I couldn't question this gift of mine anymore. Eventually my skepticism died, and I regained the belief I'd had as a child.

Skeptics have to find their own way and their own beliefs. I used to think that it was my mission to change people's minds, but after engaging in that struggle for so long, I decided it wasn't worth it. It was more important to me to focus on those who needed help with closure and healing and were open to receiving it. As soon as I made that decision, it seemed that more and more skeptics came out of the woodwork, telling me that because I didn't force my opinion on them, they were more inclined to believe. I now know that I am not here to try to change others' minds. Converting skeptics is a fantastic feeling; but ultimately, if my readings help them or others around them, then I've done the work I was put on this Earth plane to do.

◌

I encounter people who happen to be skeptical at my live shows all over the world. When I offer to do a reading for these individuals, they'll tell me up front that they're skeptical, being honest and open about it. My answer is always the same: "As long as you have an open mind, and you're ready to accept the information I'm about to give you, then that is all that matters to me."

As an example of how powerful it is for someone who's been a skeptic to turn around and finally believe, I'd like to share a reading that was featured on my TV show *Lisa Williams: Life Among the Dead*. A man was attending one of my talks with his mother, who let me know that her son was very skeptical. After the reading, however, his opinion changed dramatically. The information he received was accurate, and because it was, it helped his whole family heal deeply from a terrible tragedy.

Here is the transcript of the reading:

> LISA: I have a brother figure in Spirit here. He's saying, *I'm the brother. I'm the brother.* You shared a lot, you and your brother.
>
> MAN: Yes, it's true. We did everything together when we were younger.
>
> LISA: He wants to say hello to Mom.
>
> MAN: Mom is sitting right there. [pointing across the aisle from him]

LISA: He loves you very much, and he passed very quickly. *Dad is with me,* he's saying. Your brother acknowledges that he was warned, and there is a feeling that he placed himself in a situation of danger, that he was foolish.

MOM: Yes, he did, he did.

LISA: *I should have listened. I should have listened.* . . . Did he get shot in the head, because I keep feeling here . . . ? [pointing to her head]

MAN: He was murdered in a drive-by shooting. And yes, he was shot in the head. Half of his head was blown off.

LISA: Oh, I'm so sorry. [sighs and pauses] Do you know who Jim is?

MOM: Oh God! [shaking her head]

MAN: Jim left right after it happened. He moved away.

MOM: I want to ask a question: Is my son with my daughter? She just died, too.

LISA: Your daughter had blonde hair, and here she comes. Oh, hello!

AUDIENCE AND MOM: [laughter]

LISA: Oh, she's a little one, she's just swanned down and she's smiling radiantly, I'm looking up at her at the top of the stairs. Has she been gone for two . . . ? I'm not sure if it's two weeks or two months.

MAN: It's been about two months.

LISA: [jumping up and down] She's laughing and happy. They are together.

MOM: [happy but still pondering] About Jim . . . here's the thing. He was at the hospital before we were, and then he left and moved out of town. He may have known who did it and was afraid to tell. . . .

MAN: I have to be honest: I didn't believe. I only hoped for my mom that something would come through. Everything you said, you are 100 percent right on. This is a life-changing experience—you've changed all of our lives.

This family had gotten closure, even though the murder of their son and brother was still unsolved, and they were able to believe because the information they received was so accurate. They could now be comforted that their loved ones had made it to the Afterlife together and were happy. This is the best possible outcome for a reading, and it makes what I do so worthwhile.

CHAPTER 3

RELIGION AND SPIRITUALITY

In addition to skepticism and cynicism, there is another reason why people doubt the work of psychics and mediums. Due to their religious beliefs, many men and women are unable to accept that anything a psychic or medium has to say could possibly be true. My own experience has shown me how a person's belief in God—or the lack of it—can color his or her perspective of the spirit realm. However, I've been surprised to find that my work is actually quite congruent with the views of some of the most religious individuals I've met.

Although my father was an atheist, I attended a Church of England school. At assembly every day, students listened to different teachers talk about lessons from the Bible, and then stood up and sang hymns. In addition, the local vicar from St. Peter's Church came to talk to us once a month; occasionally, we even had visits from the Gideons, members of a group that shares the Bible worldwide, and who gave all of us students our own copy.

It was at this point that I started to take an interest in the Christian religion, not because it was forced upon me at school, but because I genuinely wanted to. However, by the time I reached the age of 13, being interested in religion was not the coolest thing you could do in your friends' eyes, so I kept it to myself. As I've already mentioned, I was never Miss Popular, and the fact that I'd sometimes say things that came true was already weird enough without my interjecting information about God and the Lord Jesus Christ.

Regardless, it became my mission in life to read the Bible cover to cover, and I dreamed of becoming a nun. At night I'd lie in bed with my little red Bible that the Gideons had given me and get totally lost in the archaic language. The stories from the Bible always sounded so interesting when the teachers at school talked about them, but I soon realized that the teachers had adapted those stories to make them appeal to our age group, and the actual thing was anything but interesting.

I could never tell my family about my interest in the Bible or of my dream of becoming a nun. My father, for one, would have had a huge problem with such a revelation. As for my mom's side of the family, her own mother spoke to dead people, and her late father had been a skeptic, so enough drama there. To add to the complications, I'd read in the Bible that mediums were not highly regarded by God at all—so the fact that my grandmother worked as a medium was clearly "wrong."

So here I was having visions, dreams, and visitations from dead spirits, yet I also wanted to be a nun. Somehow it didn't all quite fit. *I* didn't fit. There were many times I wished I weren't alive so that I could just go "back home." I never understood why the Afterlife felt like home for me; I just knew that there was an Afterlife, which I could definitely remember, and it felt safe. There, I could communicate with Spirit freely in a way I couldn't with my family members or my peers.

Finding God in Two Realms

As an adult, I came to realize that religion is a very touchy subject for people, especially for those who believe absolutely in the Bible and everything that it stands for. As a result of my work, I've come to question the view of the Bible more and more when it comes to psychic awareness and communication with the Afterlife.

The one thing that is a common thread in many religions is that there *is* an Afterlife, and all religions seem to agree that if you live the way you're supposed to according to their rules, you'll be blessed with eternal life. So, if there is an "eternal life," doesn't that point to people existing in some kind of Afterlife? And if they're there, why is it so impossible to believe that they'd want to communicate with the living?

Nevertheless, the Bible states that practices of mediums, psychics, and the occult are Satan's way of leading us astray. We should seek the truth from God, and by seeking answers from a medium or psychic, we are turning away from the true faith in Jesus and not obeying the word of the Bible. However, I began to see that the psychic and religious realms actually had a lot in common.

A reading I did for a man who was the head of a church choir helped me realize that spirituality and the Christian faith don't always have to be so opposed. When the choir director called to book an appointment, he was very polite and clearly expressed what his beliefs were, openly stating that he was unsure about having a reading because of his religion. I totally understood this and respected his honesty—I wasn't going to force the issue. In fact, I told him that he could make up his mind on the day of the appointment, and if he wanted to cancel, to please give me a courtesy call. He insisted on paying me up front so that I wasn't out of pocket if he didn't arrive. He'd be driving more than 250 miles to see me, so I knew that this wasn't a decision he was taking lightly.

When this man arrived for his reading, I could see that he was nervous, so I asked him if he'd like a cup of tea—being English, I believe that a cup of tea can solve the world's problems. He smiled and accepted my offer.

I began the reading, which turned out to be quite amazing. The choir director dropped his reserve and opened up as we connected with his mother, about whom he felt a tremendous amount of guilt, believing that he had let her down in so many ways. In the reading, he got to have the final conversation with her that he was looking for. Having achieved some closure—as well as finding a modicum of peace and comfort—his healing process had finally begun.

At the end of the session, the man asked me if I remembered our initial conversation, and how he'd told me that his religion forbade communication with the Afterlife through mediums. When I replied that I did, what came out of his mouth next shocked me. He said that on that morning, he'd gotten up early for his prayers and asked God for a sign to tell him if he should or shouldn't come to see me. He told me that God had indeed given him a sign (I didn't ask what it was) that he was supposed to have this experience, as getting a reading from me was the only way he would find the closure with his mother he'd been seeking for years.

When the choir director left, he gave me the biggest hug and said, "Never turn your back on your gift. God gave it to you for a reason—do Him proud."

During the many meditations and practices that I've done in preparation for my work and for writing this book, I've been shown that there certainly is a God, something I will discuss in depth in a later chapter. I believe that my gift is God given, and that I have it for a reason, just as all of us have some unique gift in life. It's up to us to work with it and use it. Some of us may be healers, artists, or singers; the list is endless. We have these gifts to help others, so why would we be blessed with them if they weren't to be used? But what matters is *how* we use them: if we do so with good intentions, then we will be guided to do the right thing.

The Coming Together of Spirituality and Religion

In our collective humanity, we're starting to stand on our own and find our own belief systems, and we're increasingly looking within for our own answers and guidance. This is why so many of us are starting to develop our individual gifts. The skeptics out there are becoming fewer in number, while there are more and more believers. Even those who are religious are starting to understand that spirituality and psychic ability can work hand in hand with more traditional religions.

Although spirituality has been associated with religion for many years, we are now broadening our views on that relationship. We are starting to associate both religion and spirituality with personal growth and discovery through meditation, prayer, and contemplation; while moving away from more structured religious practices and dogma.

I remember the first time I had a candid conversation with my hairstylist, who is a "born again" Christian. I was really nervous to talk so openly with her, since she's a Christian and I'm a medium. I worried that there could be a clash of opinions, but to my surprise, there wasn't. We've gone on to have many long discussions on the topic of spirituality, including why she drifted away from her church (she found the structure too imposing). She said she feels that as long as you have God in your heart and are faithful to Him, then you can deal with the rest on your own. She also told me that God is a spirit—in other words, she believes that the spirit realm exists, and she doesn't doubt what I do. Our beliefs are ultimately very similar.

In our most recent conversation, I asked her opinion about my line of work. She explained that unlike a medium, she works prophetically with God, meaning that she talks to Him directly, instead of through another person. She accepts that I have a gift and am working in the same way, although I refer to my connection as being with *Spirit* rather than with *God*. I walked away from our conversation feeling that I'd been given a sign that my gift was indeed from God.

There have been many times when the purity of my gift has come into question. This has especially been the case when crowds of religious protesters have gathered outside of the large theaters where I've been giving readings, because they believed that I was forming a cult. I must admit, I have chuckled to myself about this, but I've also been able to see their point of view: these individuals have felt strongly enough to come out and bless and pray for the souls of the people who walked past them on their way into the theater. I've been touched by this and, once onstage, I've thanked them for praying for all of our souls. I wanted to acknowledge them for making the effort to stand up for something that they believed in so strongly, knowing full well the courage this can take.

I have encountered religious opposition to my work many times. The first time I had to deal with it was when two Jehovah's

Witnesses arrived on my doorstep to discuss their beliefs. One of the ladies was rather rude when I politely told her that we had different opinions; as she pressed the issue, I explained that I worked as a medium. That was like a red flag to a bull.

The lady's friend was very sweet and calm, however, and actually taught me something that day. "If I hadn't been brought up to believe in my religion, then maybe I would believe in your work," she said. "But to me, as long as you have a belief, then that is all that matters." She said all this with a smile on her face, and then asked if she could read a passage from her Bible. I consented, and it was lovely.

This experience taught me that we are all entitled to our own beliefs, which is why I've taken the stand the way I have whenever there have been religious protesters outside of my shows. I surrender to the fact that I can't do anything to change others' minds. I don't even want to. As long as people have a belief in something, as the Jehovah's Witness lady alluded to, it will also help them believe in themselves and others.

Skepticism, cynicism, fundamental religious beliefs—all of these can make communicating with Spirit difficult. But the one thing that holds true is that we have to determine for ourselves what our own beliefs are and then act in accordance with them. We cannot allow ourselves to be controlled or ruled by outside influences—whether they be society, our parents, or the institutions we were born into—because then we're not being true to ourselves, and we'll constantly feel as if we haven't fulfilled our own journeys and pathways through life.

Thus, as you continue reading, your challenge is to closely examine your own opinions and biases, along with their source, so you can clearly make up your own mind about the reality of communicating with spirits in the Afterlife. Only *you* can do that, and I invite you to do so now.

CHAPTER 4

WHY WE FEAR DEATH—AND DON'T HAVE TO

Someone once told me that if someone comes to you with an important question about anything in life, then he or she is prepared to hear the answer. This coincides with my belief that we actually already know the answers to our important questions— we're only asking to get confirmation that our intuition is correct and that we're on the right path for our journey.

When individuals come to me with concerns about their loved ones who have passed, I know that even though they may intuit the answers, they're also seeking reassurance or comfort from the messages that come through. Those left behind want to know if their loved ones were aware that they were dying, or whether they were in any pain. Or their questions are of a personal nature, such as, "Did he know I was there in the room with him?" or "Did she know I missed her passing by only five minutes?" People especially second-guess their own reactions, asking, "Did I do the right thing? Should I feel guilty that I didn't make it to the funeral or memorial?"

Having given so many readings over the years, I can now see more similarities in them than differences. Underlying most questions I'm asked is this concern: *Is my loved one all right?* But once this issue is handled, clients seem to want to know more about what we face after passing from this life. They worry, *Does my life continue, or is this it? Do I no longer exist; does nothing survive?* Yet these queries simply point to the bigger question that just about everyone who is alive has, and that is: *Should I be afraid to die?*

A Natural, Human Fear

It's only normal to fear death, especially when you've lost someone or are facing the transition yourself. You've probably heard it said that there are only two things that are certain in life: death and taxes. This is true, and most of us don't like to think about either of them. However, just as we all came into the world, we all have to leave it. The fantasies about being bitten by a vampire and living eternally with your soul mate are all very romantic, but immortality isn't the only way to hold on to someone you love. You *will* see your friends and family members in the Afterlife, and therefore have a chance to love them once again.

Mediums and psychics aren't immune from this fear of death either. When my Nan Frances was close to the end of her life, she was taken to the hospital, where she lapsed into a coma for days. During this time, I sat at her bedside and was somehow able to tap into her soul. Knowing what my grandmother was thinking—and that she was afraid to pass—was strange for me because I was still a bit "in the closet" about my own abilities. I knew that being able to communicate with her was a part of my gift, but I hadn't explored other possibilities inherent in that gift and had generally kept quiet about it. I knew that if I told my mother the information I was getting from Nan, Mom would be upset . . . especially since there was already a lot of family drama swirling around the situation at the hospital.

I wonder why there tends to be so much turmoil when someone passes. Of course, personal experience (from readings and my own life) has helped me see a few reasons why people might become embroiled in conflict at this time. Stress is the first one. It's difficult enough to see a loved one suffer and have to face transitioning to the other side, but family members and close friends also have to deal with the fact that they're losing someone very special to them. Unfortunately, the situation gets tense, tempers flare, and arguments occur—all of which is very normal. Everyone is naturally thinking ahead to what life is going to be like, and each person deals with it in his or her own way.

Family members also have differing opinions on how to handle legal, medical, and financial issues, often feeling that they're acting in the best interest of others without realizing that they're actually *forcing* their point across. This, of course, can lead to many disputes, involving a widening circle of relatives. It's a very common scenario, and when you look at the same things from an outsider's point of view, you see them very differently.

Then you have situations in which people aren't trying to make decisions for the benefit of others, but are acting purely out of their own self-interest. Some unscrupulous individuals are thinking solely about family heirlooms, jewelry, and other items of inheritance that they've had their eye on. Sadly, this happens quite a bit, leading to behaviors and actions that cause interpersonal strife.

To avoid all of this, love should be the one thing you remain connected to. When you act out of love for the person passing, whether your actions are taken the right way or not, everyone benefits.

∽

During the time my Nan was in a coma and I was communicating with her soul, I felt very alone and cut off, much like my feelings of isolation as a child. Again, I knew I couldn't tell anyone for fear of upsetting those around me. I had no idea that it would take so long for me to understand what my grandmother had experienced before she finally left the Earth plane.

Six years after Nan Frances passed, I did a reading for a woman named Jill, who nervously clutched her cell phone the entire time. She told me that she was awaiting an urgent call, and if it came during the reading, she'd have to leave at once. I totally understood—in fact, this wasn't the first time a client came to me gripping a cell phone—and I assured her that she could go whenever she needed to.

As I focused on receiving a message for Jill, I began to get an energy coming in on my left side. I normally pick up messages from my right, so this was unusual. I started to tell Jill that I had her father-in-law with me and that he wanted to let her know he was okay, that he had left his body temporarily and was actually watching everyone from afar. He expressed that she should tell everyone that he was feeling fine, and that it was only "a matter of time" before he passed.

Jill had been crying and checking her phone every few minutes, but when I gave her this information, she stopped, looked around, and asked, "Are you really here?" Her father-in-law answered, *Yes, but I don't like these pajamas.* Jill gave a deep shudder and sigh, and told me that the call she was waiting would be letting her know if her father-in-law, who was in a coma, had passed away. She knew that he hated the pajamas he was wearing in the hospital, but they were the only ones his wife had been able to find when she was hurriedly leaving their house. The call never came during our reading, but a few days later, Jill phoned to tell me that he had indeed passed.

I learned from my reading with Jill that when a person is in a coma, the soul is released from the body to go where it may. The purpose of the soul's release in this way is twofold: either to allow the body to heal and recover (in which case, the soul will return when the body is healed), or because the soul is about to embark on its journey into the Afterlife. The silver cord that ties the body and soul together may have broken at this point, but the soul does not completely leave the body until the body has taken its last breath and the heart has stopped beating.

When my Nan lay dying and in a coma, I didn't know that her soul had started on its journey and that she had begun to deal with her fear of what would happen in the transition process. I knew from what she'd told me a few years earlier during a reading she did for me—"If I see my own death, I'm going to stop"—that she was scared of the inevitable. At the time, I didn't give this a second thought. But later, sitting by her deathbed, I knew that she was pleading not to die, repeating her earlier fear about crossing over into the Afterlife.

Nan's reaction as she passed seemed strange to me, since it came from a woman who'd had daily connections with souls in the Afterlife through the many readings she'd done over the years. She was someone who'd stood up before large audiences and worked the platform in many spiritual churches, providing evidence and facts that life continued after death. Now here she was—afraid of dying!

I couldn't accept this about her at the time, but looking back, I realize that this was due to my own immaturity. As I got older and went through my own near-death experience (NDE), I came to understand that even though we mediums know for certain that life continues, the actual transition can be a worrisome thing. It is natural and human to fear the unknown.

We all have to face the reality that at some point in life we must deal with death—whether because someone in our world is passing, or because we're facing the transition ourselves. Either way, that's one of the reasons why I decided to write *The Survival of the Soul*. My aim is to ease the fear of the unknown that just about everyone carries within. I want to assure all of you that not only *is* there an Afterlife, but there is also nothing to fear about death. Understand that when you die depends on your soul and the lessons you have already decided to learn, as well as the lessons those around you need to learn from your passing.

Nan continued to hold on in her coma for a while; unfortunately, she remained desperately afraid despite her years of daily communication with souls who had passed on. Visiting her as she lay in her hospital bed got me thinking about death and the possibility of an Afterlife, especially on my long rides home after seeing her. Mine were the normal questions that everyone asks: *Will I see my family in the Afterlife? Is there a white light? Is it going to hurt? What do you do all day in the Afterlife? Is there really life after death, or is this it?*

I did end up receiving the answers to these questions . . . so I will share what I've learned with you within these pages.

Nan Lets Go

Nan Frances showed me that it's not dying itself that frightens people—it's the leap into the unknown that marks our transition from earthly existence into the Afterlife. Nan has since helped me see a fuller picture of what I initially experienced with her as she was about to transition. That picture is fascinating and very raw in content, and it came through when I encountered her during my own NDE (described in a later chapter), as well as in readings when she spoke directly to me.

To understand the fear experienced by my grandmother, you need to know a bit more about her. Nan had an incredibly bubbly, outgoing personality, characterized by a zest for life that I've rarely seen in other people. In her later years, she traveled the globe—even a heart attack on a Mexican cruise didn't stop her! Her joy and laugh were infectious; and she radiated love, warmth, strength, and passion. These positive qualities continued right up until the end.

She also continued to drink. Not heavily, but I often came across miniature bottles of alcohol in her purse. She'd go to bingo with my mom and pour herself a gin and tonic right from her private stash. And she loved to go dancing on a Saturday night and just have fun . . . all the way up until that fateful day when she was taken to the hospital, and I got the phone call letting me know that she had lapsed into a coma.

Although Nan was certainly an incredible woman, I wasn't very close to her growing up. This was only because my mom didn't drive, and there was a considerable distance between our two homes. However, when I became independent and had my own transportation, I frequently popped in to see her. I found Nan to be a stylish woman with a social life to be envied, someone who received frequent invitations to interesting gatherings from a seemingly endless list of friends. Let's just say that she loved life and life loved her.

Because she'd been working as a medium for years, clients traveled from all over the U.K. to see her, and she flew all over the world to see them. She believed so much in her work that in many ways it took over her life. And she was so well known in the area that, even to this day, people still talk about her and her readings.

Nan Frances not only had the gift of mediumship, but she also had a highly attuned psychic awareness and often made predictions about the future. She was also regularly visited by spirit healers who helped her overcome the many ailments she'd taken on from clients—a result of not grounding and protecting herself properly while working with them.

One night Nan was visited by her team of healers, who told her that she only had 18 months left to live and there was nothing they could do about it. Now, being told you're going to die by a doctor is one thing, but hearing it from the spirit guides who know your life's path is something else! Doctors can get these types of things wrong, but it's impossible for spirit guides to do so.

This information about her time of passing terrified my grandmother, as she wasn't prepared to face death quite yet. I'm sure that as time moved on, the thought never left her mind and grew heavy on her heart. This was why she'd told me that if she saw her own death while she read for me, she'd have to stop. She knew that she only had a certain amount of time to live, and she simply didn't want to know the details.

Nan Frances suddenly went from enjoying life and sharing her exuberance with so many different people to facing the unknown, and it was a big change. She didn't want to leave her life; she enjoyed it too much. Even when her body was failing her toward the end, she still loved hearing the laughter in the hospital ward and the sounds of her family around her. She never lost sight of the joy in life.

When I visited her for the last time, she was unconscious. I asked the nurse what my Nan's chances were for pulling through, and she said they were slim. I had to face the fact that I was going to lose my beloved grandmother.

In our soul-to-soul communication, I asked Nan why she was still holding on, and I heard her reply, *I'm scared*. I placed my hand on hers and started to stroke it. I didn't know if she could hear my thoughts, so I spoke them out loud without worrying about upsetting the people around us. There had been enough family drama at that point, and I figured that my speaking to Nan as she lay in a coma wouldn't make much of a difference.

As I stroked her hand, I told her not to be scared—she could let go and join her friends and family members in the Afterlife, where they would take care of her and show her the ropes. I didn't know if I was saying the right thing, but I remember seeing a tiny twitch of a smile on her face and feeling a slight movement in her hand, possibly indicating that she'd heard me. Then my mother arrived to join the vigil, and I felt that I had to leave. The energy was so very heavy, and I needed to be alone. It was the last time I saw my grandmother alive. She passed away two days later.

From her long experience as a medium, Nan knew that there was an Afterlife and that she was going to be okay, but the anticipation of the crossing-over phase had been the cause of her greatest anxiety.

As I said before, hers was a very human reaction, and most of us have it. Imagine jumping off a high diving board for the first time and not knowing if the water is going to be cold or if you're going to land hard. The plunge into something totally alien is enough to cause anyone a good deal of apprehension.

It may be in our nature to fear the unknown, but tackling those things in life that we know little about tends to give us a great sense of accomplishment. We usually look back and say, "Well, that wasn't as bad as I expected." With respect to our transition to the Afterlife, the same thing holds true: we will move on, and we will enjoy it. Since I actually experienced it in my own NDE, trust me when I tell you that the transition to the Afterlife is an incredible and even joyous journey—one of great beauty, safety, and pure love.

Knowing When You Will Pass

When our souls make the transition from being in the body to being out of it, we frequently know beforehand that the transition is about to occur. All of us actually know when we're going to pass. You see, before we came to the Earth plane, we made an agreement to experience certain situations and circumstances, including how and when we're going to die. However, once we're here, many of us choose not to tap into our subconscious and find out when we'll be making the transition from this lifetime. It takes a strong person to accept that information and face knowing when and how his or her passing is going to happen.

A warning: if you *do* decide to access this information, which is what I did, then you may end up getting criticized when you share your knowledge with others. Ever since the book *The Secret* popularized the belief that whatever we visualize and project into the universe is going to occur, people are hesitant to make (or even hear!) radical statements that might come true. The old saying "Be careful what you wish for; you might just get it" embodies the belief that if you tell others when and how you're going to pass, they'll think you're projecting it and making it happen. However, such a concern is irrelevant, as you already know all about your own passing on a deeper level.

As Ben, my master spirit guide, says, *If we wish, we can draw on any amount of information through tapping into our own soul's knowing.* And here are the words he's used to convey the truth about what we all know, as well as how to access that knowledge:

> *Within our own way, we all know the answers to the questions that we seek . . . it is quite simple. We have the knowledge before we come here to our earthly existence. We have been given the way forward and the answers that we need; we just have to look deep within ourselves and know that they are there. Similar to reading hidden messages that are encrypted, we have only to uncover the meaning of the code to unlock a vast amount of knowledge and information.*

Ben goes on to describe how we can uncover the meaning of the code:

> *Meditation is the key that opens the door to all the knowledge and understanding in life—certainly to our current lives and also to the many other lives we have led before.*

What Ben is alluding to is that your soul made an agreement in the Afterlife, called a "Life Contract," before you returned to your current earthly existence. Therefore, you actually have all the answers within for whatever you set out to accomplish and experience in your life. Meditation is the key.

Having full awareness of your time of passing can be a blessing and a curse. I've been known to look at people, either face-to-face or via a recent photo, and know when they're going to die. Even if the individual happens to be aware of this information as well, it is never an easy message to deliver or receive.

Students of mine who are trying to develop their own psychic or mediumship abilities often complain that they only get negative messages, such as about an illness or when someone is going to die. In spite of their desire to receive more positive messages, we all have different gifts—some of us simply have a better way of communicating negative information to others, so we only get that kind of information. It doesn't mean that a person can't develop further, but rather that each man or woman is only given information that is needed and will be of help.

I'm often asked, "Before we die, do we get any warning that we are going to pass?" To answer that question, let's take a closer look at the actual time period before the passing phase occurs. Some people might be told by a doctor how much time they have left, and have their death sentence hanging over them like a time bomb ticking away. Others have no such warning, and death happens quite suddenly. Ask yourself this: do you want to know the date of your passing and be able to say your good-byes, or would you rather just leave and not have to face knowing the time and circumstances?

Although we all know when we're going to die, most of us ultimately choose not to become conscious of that information. With that said, there are times when you can be aware that something is going to happen, usually signaled by a shift in feeling or a vague sense of knowing. There are many examples of this, including one that occurred during a reading I did for the parents of a boy who had died in a freak boating accident.

Jordan had not wanted to go on his family's boat that day, but his parents insisted. He was clearly frightened, having a sense that *something* was going to happen. When I spoke with his parents, they expressed much guilt that they'd forced their son to join them on the boat. But in the greater scheme of things, Jordan's life was scheduled to end at that time and in that place, having been arranged during his contract before birth. If he hadn't passed in that particular boating accident, his passing would have happened in another way.

The following transcript of the reading that took place will help you see how Jordan knew he was going to pass as a result of the accident:

> LISA: He is calling it a freak accident and wants to say to his dad, *Please don't feel guilty, because I knew it was coming.* He is showing me that for weeks, he was preparing both of you for this event.
>
> MOM: After he'd passed away, we found something he'd written on MySpace, and I wondered about it.
>
> LISA: He knew he was going to pass.
>
> MOM: Did he know? Did he have a notion in the back of his mind?
>
> LISA: He knew.
>
> DAD: On the MySpace message board, he wrote who his hero was. It was supposed to be my name [laughs and smiles], but instead he wrote the name *Jesus*.
>
> MOM: And after that, he wrote, *I'll be seeing you soon.* Not, *I'll be seeing you someday,* which might be expected if he were planning to live a full life. And then he finished by writing, *Until then, much love.* This was kind of strange to us.

Jordan had indeed had a sense that his passing was imminent for a while. He didn't *consciously* know but had instead tapped into his subconscious, and the information that came to the surface caused him to write his cryptic message on MySpace.

∽

There are other ways information about your unavoidable passing may be revealed, such as through your intuition. Your spirit guides and loved ones can also tell you directly, often through your dreams. These dreams will be exceptionally vivid, making you feel as if you were really being visited by your loved ones. (Such lifelike visitations don't necessarily mean that you're soon to pass, so don't worry if you're having them.) Or you might be awake and see the spirit of someone very close to you, but that spirit will look like a real person. Again, there are many of us who see spirits in this way, so don't think that just because you are seeing a spirit, you are going to pass. The reading I had with Amanda will illuminate the difference.

Amanda had lost her grandmother only a year before she came to see me. The older woman had passed suddenly while in the hospital, and Amanda felt a need for closure. Although she genuinely wanted to connect with her grandmother and some other family members, she was nervous about the reading because she didn't know what to expect.

My new client explained that before her grandmother had passed, she'd been sitting up in her hospital bed looking well. Amanda had come to collect her, but they had to wait for the doctors to sign the discharge paperwork. The two women were chatting when the grandmother unexpectedly exclaimed, "Oh, look! There's your granddad. He's got that white light behind him that people talk about when someone dies."

Amanda, whose granddad had died about 15 years earlier, asked her grandmother what she was seeing. "Oh, can't you see him, dear?" the older woman said. "Well, I can, clearly. I wonder what he wants."

Amanda's grandmother stared at the corner of the room where she was seeing her late husband. The young woman sensed that the room had gotten a bit chilly, but she didn't think anything about it at the time. She couldn't see anything, and she thought that it was simply wishful thinking on her grandmother's part to be seeing her dead husband again.

Suddenly, her grandmother announced, "Oh, he wants me to go with him! I think I'm leaving you soon."

Amanda wasn't happy to hear this; after all, she was there to take the older woman home after a successful minor surgery.

"You're not going anywhere yet," she told her grandmother. "The doctors wouldn't let you go if you were about to die!"

An hour or so passed, with the two of them laughing and talking about the latest scandals on their favorite soap operas, when Amanda was called out to the nurses' station to sign her grandmother's release forms. Amanda left the older woman, now dressed and sitting in a chair with her knitting, for five minutes . . . only to return and find her still sitting in the chair but with the knitting needles on the floor, her eyes closed, and a smile on her face. She had passed away during those few minutes when Amanda had been gone!

I confirmed in Amanda's reading that her grandmother was being guided to go with her husband, and that she was happy to do so. She came through and said, *He was motioning for me to go to him and had his arms out straight. They were so welcoming. He looked good, not like he did when I last saw him. He looked like he was about 35, all handsome and dashing.* She told me that as she sat in the hospital room, she had closed her eyes, hoping to pull her husband closer to her, and then she smiled because she found herself in his arms. Although her death certificate noted that she passed due to natural causes, truth be told, it was just her time to go—and she did so with knowledge and volition, happy to be reunited with her husband again.

My Grandfather's Passing

Much like Amanda's grandmother, my paternal grandfather passed with an awareness of what was to come. I also had the feeling that he was leaving—and as I look back on that event, I can see that certain behaviors and interactions that puzzled me at the time now make perfect sense.

Shortly before the time of his transition, I'd been on Granddad's case for weeks to clean up the corner of the dining room where he kept all of his old newspapers, in what appeared to be random stacks. Granddad loved horse racing; although he'd place a bet or two, he wasn't a huge gambler, normally spending only 50 pence (about 75 cents) each way for a horse. But he'd study the racing form for hours, and he'd collect and keep all the newspapers so that he could do his research.

Finally, one day he called me up and said, "Ay, Lis, guess what I've done? I've cleared the dining room so you and your grandmother can stop nagging me," and he laughed. I went over that weekend, and indeed he had cleaned the mess up—it was so tidy! My grandmother was over the moon at the sudden change in his behavior, thrilled to have some space back in the dining room.

A week later, my grandfather went into the hospital with a minor chest infection, something that had happened before and never turned out to be very serious. It was a Friday afternoon when I got a call on my cell phone. Without even looking at the number, I told a colleague, "Oh, that's my grandmother telling me that Granddad is in the hospital with his chest problem again." That's just what it was. When I answered, my grandmother told me not to worry, that he would be fine. Granddad just needed an IV for antibiotics and would be out by Monday.

On Saturday afternoon, I went to pay him a visit. As I walked from the car to the hospital entrance, I felt a peculiar heavy energy around me and knew that something was going to happen. I walked in to see my grandfather sitting up in bed with family and friends surrounding him, entertaining them with his endless jokes and even flirting with the nurses by winking at them—all of which proved to me that he was back to his normal self.

But still . . . something wasn't sitting right with me, and this feeling increased every time my granddad looked at me. His gaze was penetrating, as if he were looking through my body and into my soul. It was an incredible sensation. I still remember the moment I went to say good-bye and looked into his eyes one last time. It was as if his human consciousness stopped, and his soul, the true essence of him, took over just for a split second—but it was long enough for me to recognize what was happening.

At that moment, I connected with Granddad's soul. His eyes were bright blue and crystal clear. As the saying goes, "The eyes are the windows of the soul," which is so true. We looked at each other with a sense of total connection. He knew it was the last time he'd see me, and he held my gaze longer than usual, savoring the sight before him. I didn't break that gaze either, feeling that I was communicating with him on a deeper level with no words needed.

At one point, I felt an impulse to say "I love you," but since our family was not comfortable with emotion, for me to say those words would have alarmed everyone around me. And since by that time they all knew I was psychic, they would have wondered what was going on. Instead, I *thought* the words, and I could tell by his silent acknowledgment that he got my message.

I had never experienced such a powerful connection with a soul before, nor have I since, and I doubt I ever will; it was utterly indescribable. The energy around my grandfather was so clear, shimmering, and radiant. It was then that I understood on a deeper level what was happening—that this was the last time I would see him alive.

As my grandmother walked me out of the hospital ward, she told me that Granddad was being released the next day, and that he was looking so much better. I have no idea where the words came from, but I blurted out, "No, there is more to come."

My grandmother looked puzzled upon hearing my words. "No, he's looking so much better," she countered. I found out later that when my grandfather was being loaded into the ambulance, he'd tried to tell her where important documents concerning the house and other finances were located. She wouldn't hear of it, insisting, "Oh, Jack, don't be silly! You'll be out in a few days!"

The day after my visit, Granddad died of an embolism in the stomach due to a change in the medication that the hospital had given him. When I was sorting through all the legal documents later, I noticed that he had bound together and dated some papers. These were dated the day he'd called to tell me that he'd cleaned out the dining room. On one of the papers, he'd highlighted the words: *In the event of my death, please call . . .* He obviously knew that his time was near.

People often start to get their "house in order" when approaching their time of transition. They look at their life-insurance policies, finalize financial paperwork, or make sure to have their will taken care of. This is because they have a subconscious awareness of what is going to happen, just as my grandfather had.

How Spirit Prepares Us

Seeking more information on the process of how we can know that the time of passing is near, I meditated and received the following message from Ben—my fingers typing as fast as I could in order to capture as much as possible. I share that here, with much gratitude for Ben and the rest of my team:

> Before you pass, we prepare you for your journey ahead. While you sleep, you travel astrally, visiting others in your dreams to get used to the process. You look at situations and people you love, and you visit the places you have always wanted to go. We guide you in this, which is why many individuals report wild and vivid dreams before passing.
>
> For a month or so before you pass, we prepare you very gently, placing situations around you to help in the process. Whether you are going to pass through natural causes, a car accident, or a murder, you will have fulfilled your reason for being on the Earth plane and completed your contract. Still, we have to prepare you slowly. We also have to prepare your loved ones on the other side to receive you. A lot goes into receiving a soul over to us, as we have to make sure that everyone here is ready to take on their role. But be assured that we follow you and guide you, knowing when your passing is going to happen.
>
> You may not choose to leave when there is an exit point, or you may choose to leave before it is your time. If you choose to leave before your time, we send you back, as in a "near-death experience," because you did not fulfill your purpose on Earth. There are souls who make choices about their passing that we cannot control; however, this is not something we need to look at now, but will be explained later.

Normally, we become closer and more active in our help two weeks before your passing. We also start to help your friends and family during that time period. One way we do so is to influence you to make calls and write letters to loved ones, and also to tidy up whatever you have lying around—the material issues that go with life—so that you are not worrying about leaving a mess behind.

So we do everything to influence and help you prepare, but we cannot force you. Some people do not want to follow our lead, and we accept that. But it will be harder on them when they do come over here, because with little or no preparation for transition, they may find themselves in a state of shock upon recognizing where they are.

If you have awareness that you will soon be departing, then you may very likely see us doing our preparation work around you. The veil between worlds becomes thin when you are about to pass, and we make it even thinner by helping you raise your vibration, showing you how to do it. By raising your vibration, you are more able to let go of your earthly body. Again, this is part of the process of transition, how we prepare you for your crossing over.

If you have been told that you are facing death, it is easier for us to prepare you, because you are more willing to deal with the inevitable. Perhaps a doctor has given you information that you will die at a specific time, and you have had to face the harsh reality that it is going to happen. But if you are not given any information about when you might expect to pass, you will be harder to prepare, but not by much. You may be a little more stubborn, so we do our preparation when you are sleeping.

We help your soul come to terms with the fact that you are going to pass. We tell you what is happening, and we allow you to go where you need to and see people you need to visit. We help you with that process, which is why you know you are leaving when you are ready to pass. Your spirit guides do this for you, and because they have had a relationship with you since the beginning of your life on the Earth plane, they know what you need and what you do not need.

Three days before your passing, the intensity of the process starts to get stronger. We are around you 24/7, staying close to the veil and with you through everything. In particular, we watch your state of mind and help you become as peaceful as possible. It is essential that we are able to get you into a peaceful state, because if you are not calm and peaceful, you risk being trapped between worlds during your transition. We strive to get you into this state for many reasons, but I will cover that in more detail later so that you do not get confused.

We have to help you become calm and peaceful so we can make sure you do all you need to do before your time of transition. This is when your friends and family will start to get phone calls they do not expect, and when you start sharing emotions and thoughts with them that you may have withheld in the past. As these kinds of events unfold, everyone around you will feel the change and the transition coming, if only on a subconscious level. This is why so often a person may have known something was going to happen but could not quite put his or her finger on what it was.

At this time we also try to clear your soul of so much weight, so you may feel like you have a new lease on life—certainly that is what you feel when you know you are finally going to cross. You will feel the freedom and exhilaration of having cut your earthly ties and obligations. Us clearing your soul is just another way to make sure that the transition is easy. We try to take away all the guilt, the hate, the fear, the anger—anything that is negative. It is not always easy, so we often do this at night when your ego isn't in the way, and we can tap into your soul. Ego is a huge thing for all of us to overcome; when we arrive on the other side, we lose the ego, but it is a tough battle on the Earth plane. At night when you sleep, your body repairs itself, and we clear and repair your soul.

Normally, around 24 hours before you pass, you start to see flashes of white light. At this point in the process of transition, all the spirits who are coming to collect you come together as a group. This is how we, as Spirit, are able to connect with you across the veil, by using all the energy that we can gather in a mass. That amount of energy has to come from many sources. You may sense us close or see us, and comment that we are in the room. In some cases, a passing person may use our energy to project an image of someone he or she recognizes, perhaps an image of someone known in life. We are all helping to get that image across to the person, which takes a lot of energy, but we have prepared for a long time to be able to offer such help to those who are transitioning and need it.

As the time of crossing grows closer, those who are ill and facing death—and know they are dying—will make a decision about when they will pass. This was the case with Lisa's Nan Frances, who at first fought her passing fiercely. She even fought me, Ben, until she finally recognized me from having been together in a former life. Even then, she still didn't want to acknowledge that she had left her body.

"Trust it to be you," she finally said when she looked at me and knew who I was. We both burst out laughing and embraced. It was a beautiful moment, because she had finally chosen to let go. If a person is struggling and refusing to pass, we have to wait until the body has failed completely—as was the case with Lisa's Nan Frances—and then we can lift the soul out of the body and through to us.

Most souls we can easily coax and it is very straightforward, but there are a few who are harder than others. The easy ones choose their time and come willingly. They decide to see us when we are close; while they are in and out of consciousness, we talk to them. They tell us whether they are ready, and when they are, we help lift the soul from the body and then sever the cord that connects the two. Often when you choose your time, you choose it because you have been given permission to leave, such as by a child who is with you, or because everyone you care about has visited you. Or you may well choose a time when friends and family members are not there, because your ego is still strong and you do not want to upset anyone. All of these choices depend on the personality and the character of the person.

Until the moment you come through the veil, you are still a person with choices, which is why you may decide when you want to leave and whom you want to wait to see. Sometimes you will not get to see everyone because your body gives up first. That is unfortunate, but your soul may still linger on until you see those you wish to see one last time.

When someone passes suddenly in what may be violent circumstances, we in Spirit know when it is going to happen; however, we do not know the exact moment, so we have to be ready for it. It is like staying alert to catch a ball that could be tossed in your direction at any time. We are then able to catch the soul when it pops out of the body, before any trauma or shock can hit the body, which is why many on this side say they did not feel anything at the moment of a fatal accident. It is hard to understand how it could be that it did not hurt, especially when death came from a shooting or a particularly violent accident. But always, when the body is going through some form of trauma or shock in the transition, the soul will remove itself to ensure that it stays complete and intact. This is not because a soul can be damaged, but because it chooses to remove itself as protection from any pain.

In the case of a suicide, it is a little more complex. We do all we can to comfort and understand the soul before this happens. Often, when the suicide is planned over a period of time, we can help in sufficiently preparing the soul for the transition. But if it is a spur-of-the-moment suicide, it may be a surprise, and we have to gather spirits quickly to help the soul over. It is not simple, but we do it, and we do it quickly. Some suicides are predestined—you made your decision long ago, often depending on what may have happened in your last life. You do this because your soul needs to have a certain experience, or you need to teach a lesson to people you are leaving behind. I know it is hard to believe, but we will discuss this more later, and it will be clearer at that time.

A Revealing Reading

Ben's teaching is clearly demonstrated in the following story based on a reading I did for a woman whose son died tragically in a motorcycle accident.

Kay came to see me shortly after her son, Chris, had passed. Chris came through to me as his usual bubbly and charming self, which pleased his mom, as you can imagine. He began by talking about his life and his accomplishments, so he could prove to her that it was really him.

Because Chris had died in a freak accident, Kay hadn't been ready to hear the details of his passing, but now she wanted to know. At the time, she'd declined to hear the police report of what had actually occurred. Without any information, she was now left with a sense of incompleteness and couldn't let go.

During the reading, Chris related a detailed account of what had happened in the accident, which was later verified by the police officers who were at the scene. It turns out that the young man had been riding on his motorcycle and had taken a corner too quickly, hitting a patch of the road that was slippery from oil left by another vehicle, which caused him to lose control. Fortunately, no one else had been involved in the incident.

Chris described the feelings that he had as he slid on his bike through the oil patch:

> CHRIS [talking through Lisa]: *I knew it was there, Mom. I knew it. I was going to lose it. I couldn't hold it. I tried, but I couldn't. You never wanted me to have the bike, and I'm sorry. But I was always careful.*
>
> [Kay nods, crying softly]
>
> CHRIS: *Well, it was strange. I lost control. It all happened really slowly, like slow motion. I started to fall, and my leg went under the bike. I was heading toward the rock wall on the bend, and I thought, Oh, shit, this is going to hurt. I went to cover my head, but next thing I knew, I was being tugged out of my body . . . and then I was flying, watching everything that was happening to my body below.*

KAY: [gasping] That's amazing, I don't know what to say. I'm shocked!

CHRIS: *I came out of my body before the impact happened, so I didn't feel a thing, Mom. Honest. It happens all the time. The spirit guides know when to come for you and to help you out, so you don't feel any pain. I was blessed. Don't cry, Mom. I love you, and please know that I am fine.*

✐

Knowing that your transition over to the Afterlife is painless and fully supported by Spirit should be of great comfort, as well as help diminish the fear of death. But exactly how that transition occurs—who greets you when you arrive, if there is a heaven or hell, and when and how you can visit your loved ones on the Earth plane—is still to be told.

In Part II, you'll discover what awaits you as you pass from earthly existence and make your journey to the other side, a process that is not only safe and painless, but a beautiful beginning of your "life after life."

✐

PART II

CROSSING OVER

CHAPTER 5

THROUGH THE VEIL

Crossing through the veil from this world to the next can be a beautiful process, one that we all face and would do well to accept and embrace. As discussed, there is nothing to fear as you pass from this world to the next; in fact, the transition can be quite thrilling. As my spirit guide Ariel says:

> *Death is like a journey into outer space: you never know what you are going to encounter. You have to embrace it and accept it. Know that it is coming no matter what you are doing in life.*

Thanks to my near-death experience (NDE), I know what it's like to cross over into the threshold of the Afterlife. The experience left me with a personal testament of what happens when we die, which I would like to share with you in this chapter.

My Journey Across—and Back

In April 2004, I was being treated for a severe infection in my fallopian tubes, when I left my body as a soul in transition. I crossed the veil and was pulled through the White Light into what awaits us all on the other side.

Many individuals have reported having had an NDE after their heart stopped beating on the operating table, or while awaiting rescue or resuscitation after an accident. Remarkably, and with few exceptions, people report experiences that closely match descriptions given by others who have also had NDEs.

In my case, there was no medically verifiable indication that I "died," as no heart monitor had been hooked up at the time. I do remember returning to my body—after having experienced the unmistakable passage, in every detail, of a soul entering the Afterlife—and hearing my partner at the time, Kevin, calling frantically for a doctor.

The day before I went into the hospital, I recall feeling and acting quite strange, sensing my spirit guide Ben around me in a very protective way. That afternoon a friend called to ask me if I wanted to go out. Normally I would have grabbed my coat and said, "Okay, where are we off to?" But this time, as I started to say "Okay," a different word came out. I actually remember forming my mouth to say "Okay," when "No" came out instead. It was as if I had lost control of my own mouth. I thought for a moment about what I'd said, and then I realized that I was actually in too much physical pain to go out. I decided to head to bed instead.

That night I had a dream featuring all of my loved ones, including my granddad and Nan Frances, and it was incredible to feel their presence. We were gathered together for a wedding—*my* wedding. Although I was dancing with a man I didn't recognize, I was surrounded by people I knew and loved dearly: my family, my spirit guides, my helpers . . . everyone in Spirit.

Suddenly, in the midst of all this celebration, I was being stabbed in the back. The pain was very real, yet I didn't know who had attacked me. I was in shock—this was my wedding, and someone was stabbing me in the back! I remember worrying that my gown was going to get stained with blood if I didn't try to save it, while the intense pain radiated outward from the wound.

I woke up with a severe, stabbing pain in the left side of my lower back. Like the wound in my dream, this pain was radiating across my body, engulfing my entire torso with a burning sensation. It was excruciating, and I couldn't bear it. I was taken to the nearest hospital, which happened to be on the campus of the University of California, Los Angeles (UCLA).

In spite of being nearly blinded by the pain, I was aware that Ben, my Nan, and my granddad were all in the car with me as I was being driven to the hospital. It wasn't just a sense of energy that gave me this awareness—I could clearly see them sitting in the backseat of the car. I could make out their shapes, expressions, hair color, eyes, and even the ways in which they moved. Each time I looked behind me at one of them, it was as if I were looking at a real person, even though I knew that it was a spirit.

There was also a soft hum in my head. When I could focus through the pain to listen to it, I made out the sound of chatter—so much chatter that it sounded like crowds of people were whispering, but quietly, as if they didn't want to be heard. It was strange, almost comforting in a way. Somehow I knew I was going to be all right.

As I was being admitted into the emergency room, I could see my three spirit visitors walking by the side of my wheelchair. Although I wondered what was going on, I figured they were there to look after me. It was not uncommon for me to see spirits when I was ill. In fact, I'd noticed over the years that my mediumship and psychic-awareness abilities were actually heightened at such times.

Little did I know that my visitors had come for a more specific purpose: to help my soul release from my body so I could bear the trauma I was about to experience.

೧೦

Lying in my hospital bed, I experienced the most severe pain of my life—it came in waves, and just kept getting stronger and stronger. It became so intense that I could no longer pay attention to the spirits who were with me; instead, I had to focus on sending healing energy to myself so that I could deal with the agony. It was too difficult to move and place my hands on myself for a healing, but I used my mind to focus as best I could.

As I poured healing energy into my body, a sense of utter calmness came over me. The panicky feeling left, and I accepted what was going on. I breathed deeply and knew that I was going to be okay. Even so, the pain was getting progressively worse, despite the increased dosages of morphine that I was being given. The relief that the drug gave me only lasted for 15 minutes, instead of the 45 minutes it was supposed to. Each time a wave of pain washed over me, it was stronger than the one before. I lay there with a searing sensation shooting through my lower abdomen for almost three hours, my body convulsing through each contraction as it came on thick and fast.

I remember thinking, *Please take me; I can't take this anymore.* Then I shut my eyes, stopped resisting, and surrendered, allowing the pain to flow through me. All of a sudden, I felt myself drifting, like I'd been cut loose from an anchor that had held me attached to my body and its distress. I wasn't drifting upward so much, as you might expect; rather, I was drifting *away.* My movement was effortless, as if I were being carried along on an invisible but powerful current. My soul was no longer trapped in my body. *I was free!*

I noticed that I was no longer in any pain. As a soul, I felt fine; in fact, I felt more than fine. I knew that if I looked back, I'd see my body lying in the bed—still, lifeless, and with an expression of anguish on my face—and I chose not to do that. I had a sense that being free from the pain would only last a short time, even though it seemed like it could be forever. I was soaring like a bird in the sky, gliding over the planet with ease. My soul was liberated.

I had the sensation that I was passing through a shimmering veil, which I recognized as the one that separates the Earth plane from the Afterlife. I felt myself being pulled through this veil as if by a magnet. As I came through, I could see a huge ball of light so bright that it would blind any human eyes. But as a soul, I didn't have physical eyes, so I "saw" the light as warm and glowing, not harsh in any way.

I seemed to be moving through a kind of tunnel that was shimmering and alive. And there, at the end of this tunnel, was the White Light, which filled my every cell with unconditional love of the purest kind. The love I felt as I passed into the White Light cannot be quantified in earthly terms, as it was so much stronger than any form of human love that you might have for a significant other or even a child.

Still floating and gliding, I came face-to-face with Nan Frances, who in life had shared my gifts and whose spirit had been present with me on the Earth plane during my current ordeal. Now she stood before me, smiling and with her arms open; as I approached,

I felt myself being embraced by her love and the love of all those who were nearby. I couldn't make out the faces of any of the others who were there with her—she was the only one I saw. I looked around for my dear granddad, but sadly I didn't see him.

Nan said, *You're not ready to see him yet.* I was shocked that she could read my thoughts, but then I realized that souls connect through thoughts, not words spoken out loud.

My grandmother was still smiling, and I noticed that she was so much younger and healthier than the last time I had seen her. She was radiant and glorious, and simply standing in her presence was indescribably wonderful. I wanted to talk to her, but as I tried to form words in my mind, she said, *Shh, don't try to talk. I need you to listen.*

For a long moment, we stared at each other. Nan looked right through me, as if she were tapping into my mind and reading all my thoughts. As we gazed at each other, my mind began to race: *Where am I? What am I doing here? Am I dead? Who are those people? Why do I hear a buzzing noise?* As all of these questions were going through my mind, Nan suddenly broke in.

It's not your time yet, she told me. *You are to go back.*

I knew what she was saying, but I didn't want to hear it. I was free of pain, and returning to my body meant that I'd have to endure that terrible agony again. I wanted to stay where I was. I knew that my son would be taken care of, that he'd be safe and well with my parents and his father. In fact, *everything* in my life would be taken care of without me, and all would go on. And since I was already in the Afterlife, didn't that mean I was supposed to stay here?

Nan's voice once again addressed my inner thoughts: *You have much work to do. You are a teacher, and you will be helping many people in your lifetime.* And then I saw a large screen before me, on which was revealed all of the things she was telling me I'd do in my life. As I took it all in, I understood what she meant—it wasn't my time to stay in the Afterlife, and I did have important work to do.

Nan Frances continued to communicate with me about the meaning of life and how my gift would help others, allowing me to interact and ask questions at times. I was shown several events and circumstances that would influence me, and also many decisions I would make. I understood everything at the time, but then I lost the memory of it when I returned. Nevertheless, the information became stored in my subconscious mind—so now when I arrive at one of those moments I was shown, I recognize it from my NDE and get a powerful déjà vu feeling, as though I've been there before. And I have!

Conversing with my Nan was strange and wonderful; it was as if the hands of time had stopped. To put it into the perspective of earthly time, I felt like I'd been with her for hours, standing in one spot with my "body" never tiring. It was such an incredible, eternal feeling. But sadness hit me when I felt Nan and all those around beginning to vanish, signaling that the incredibly rich and loving conversation was drawing to a close.

Once again, my grandmother affirmed that I would have to return to the Earth plane and be a good mother to my son, Charlie, and also become a teacher. I wasn't sure what she meant about teaching, since the original vision she'd shown me faded as I started to return. I was puzzled because even though I'd trained to be a school-teacher, I'd decided against it as a career after some brief experience in an actual classroom. (Later, Nan's message was clarified when I realized that I was to teach spiritual lessons, psychic awareness, and mediumship—and that many people would learn from me.)

I felt my grandmother and her helpers leave, and then I looked down to once again see the familiar silver cord I'd known as a child traveling out of my body. I felt the tug, and that was it. A force coming from my solar plexus sent me whooshing back, as if I were being sucked through the hose of a vacuum cleaner.

I landed hard back in my body . . . which was writhing in pain. Once again, my soul felt trapped in my physical self, an awareness I had in spite of the torture I was going through. I opened my eyes to see the digital clock on the table next to me and noticed that about one minute had passed, if even that long. Time really had stopped!

The Power of the Soul

By now, I assume that you're more comfortable with the process of transition we must all go through: the soul's passing from this life into the White Light before reaching the Afterlife. It may also be helpful for you to clearly understand just how powerful your soul is. First, let me introduce you to *who* your soul truly is.

Your soul—not your consciousness or your ego—is the very essence of who you are, so it governs every aspect of your living and dying. The soul encompasses your personality, your fear, your love, and your passion. It is also what is indestructible about you, as it can never be destroyed. People will try to break your soul, but it is too strong for any damage to be done. The strength of your soul is not a physical phenomenon; instead, it is pure energy that pulsates and radiates throughout your physical body.

Your soul holds the key to everything you will go through on Earth in the future, as well as what you've already experienced in your current life and in your past incarnations. It is magnificently powerful, so you must always honor that power and what it stands for.

Imagine, if you will, that your soul contains your personality and, through that personality, governs how your body expresses your essence. For instance, if your soul is vibrant and happy, you will be animated in expressing yourself. That's because your soul projects that happy energy to your brain, which responds by sending signals to your muscles to make your hands and face move in an animated way. This demonstrates how the soul is the true core of *who you are.*

Likewise, if you're sad and your soul is hurting, your body reacts in certain ways to express your painful emotions. Your soul governs everything about you, so there is a lot to be said for thinking positively and projecting good thoughts and emotions. If your soul believes your thoughts, then whatever thoughts you put out there will manifest and reach fulfillment. That is the power of your soul.

∽

There are several factors that come into play to determine a soul's time on, and manner of departure from, the Earth plane.

Some people pass because their "exit point" was predestined, part of a plan that was designed before birth. (I will cover the subject of predestination in a later chapter.) Everyone has several exit points in life—like a cat with nine lives—but the choice isn't always a simple one. Some of us have more exit opportunities than others, and thus have more options. Because of this flexibility, we can influence our time of passing to some degree through our will to live. For example, I have read for many individuals who fought a terminal illness and won the battle because they strongly affirmed that they would recover. And because their soul believed their thoughts and informed their body to get well, they did.

It doesn't always work that way, however. If a person facing a terminal illness appears determined to recover, the question is, does he or she *really* mean it? If not, the soul ignores the false message —and, since the body is informed by the soul, the body starts to fail. That's what happened with one client of mine.

I was the one who informed George that he was ill and should immediately seek medical attention for his symptoms, which he did. (At times like these, I take the question *Do you want to know everything?* very seriously.) It was discovered that he had bowel cancer and had been given only a few months to live.

I saw George often after his diagnosis, and used my abilities as a Reiki practitioner to transmit healing energy to him. But whenever I did so, I got the sense that something was not right with him— it was as if he didn't really believe he'd recover.

None of the people around George wanted to see him lose his battle with cancer, so he stayed positive. He made sure that his family heard him say all the right words: "I will fight this! When I get well again, I want to . . ." But as I continued to read for him and give him healing energy, I could feel his sense of defeat and knew that he was going to pass. Four weeks after I first noticed that he'd given up, my client died peacefully in his sleep.

Not long after George passed, his daughter came to see me. She said that her father had great faith in my work, and she hoped that I might help her get the closure she needed. In the reading I did for her, George appeared as his ever-vibrant self, but soon confirmed that he'd lost faith during his illness and had chosen to go. Although he'd stayed positive throughout his illness, he was only giving friends and family what they wanted, since in his soul he'd already decided to leave. He assured his daughter that he had chosen to go when he did and that it was a very peaceful transition. She was greatly relieved, as she thought he'd suffered in passing, and that it had occurred against his will.

Breaking Free into Spirit

Knowing that your soul is indestructible will help you stay strong when it's time to cross over. How your soul breaks free, and what you as a soul will then encounter, is my next subject.

As I've already mentioned, the soul is attached to your physical body through an energetic connection referred to as the silver cord. Many people who have experienced an out-of-body experience (OBE), a near-death experience (NDE), or astral-travel have reported that they saw what looked like a cord or a rope sparkling with a silvery energy stretching out from their head, chest, back, or tummy.

The silver cord is linked to each of your seven major chakras— those whirling vortices that serve as your physical body's natural energy centers. The cord is also the lifeline through which your soul feeds energy and information to your physical body, much like the umbilical cord feeds nourishment to a baby inside its mother.

As you sleep, your soul often leaves your body so your physical self can recover from illness or trauma, or so you can travel and experience important lessons. As a teacher, I often leave my body to help others understand the tenets of spirituality. It's not unusual for me to have dreams in which I meet up with someone and then learn later that this person had the same dream I did.

Since the silver cord is both flexible and durable, it can withstand a lot of astral-traveling, stretching to accommodate what may seem like a great distance. But it only allows you to go so far before pulling you back quickly, keeping you securely tethered to your body in the physical world. However, this starts to change when you're being prepared to cross over into the Afterlife.

During this transitional process, you become physically weaker, due to the lack of energy feeding your body from the soul or from the chakras that the soul is linked to. Your aura (the outward expression of your energetic body) also starts to change—and because it's associated with the major chakras, these become affected as well, further weakening the silver cord. As your soul moves up and away from your physical body, the weakened cord snaps. When this occurs, you are no longer tethered to your physical body, and death is irreversible . . . your journey has truly begun.

In tragic accidents that result in trauma and lead to death, the cord snaps, yet it often does so before any painful impact occurs. As mentioned previously, this is so the soul doesn't feel the agony that the physical body experiences at the time of sudden death. I've done many readings in which the spirit of someone came through to show how the person passed before an actual impact—as you read about in the last chapter, when I shared my reading with Kay, the mother of the young man who had died in a motorcycle accident.

When you leave your body and the cord finally snaps, there is an exhilarating feeling as the soul releases from what has confined it for so long. Sometimes the soul jumps out of the body quickly; other times, it moves out more slowly. But in either case, when the cord finally breaks, your time in this body has come to an end. Your soul is now truly free—just as a dog shakes the water from its coat, you shake off the physical body and leave it behind.

Choosing the White Light

When the cord snaps, the majority of souls head toward the veil and then on to the White Light. This is a choice made by the soul (and it was clearly what I decided to do during my NDE). Those who don't take this direction remain behind, trapped in what is known as "the vortex," a place that is neither the Earth plane nor the Afterlife. I cover the fate of those souls that remain behind more extensively in the next chapter, but here I want to describe what you can expect when you penetrate the veil and head for the White Light.

Even though the spirit world is in another dimension and time, we can still access it from within our world. In linear, spatial terms, the spirits that come through during readings are located about three feet away from us in the physical world, but they're in a different dimension of higher-vibrational frequency. So as the soul leaves the body, exiting at an angle of 20 to 30 degrees, it moves to a location about three feet away from the body. Here, the soul crosses the veil and moves into the White Light, supported all the way by spirit guides. As Josiah the Elder says:

The magical White Light would blind your human eyes, but for us it is pure love beyond any knowing, an example of what is to come.

Before you arrive at the White Light, you travel through what appears to be a tunnellike structure. It is not as you imagine a tunnel to be—dark and ominous—rather, it shimmers as if ripples of energy are running through it. Imagine looking over the hood of a car when the engine has been running on a hot day, and seeing distant objects through the haze. This is what the tunnel looks like as you move through it, marking the beginning of your journey into the spirit world. You can see a light beyond and are drawn along through the shimmering tunnel as if by a magnet, getting closer and closer to the luminous White Light ahead.

Throughout your transition, you're always able to see your loved ones waiting for you on the other side. They'll appear to be so close that you can almost reach out and touch them, but you'll be able to do so only after you've made your way through the tunnel. You may also see people you recognize from this world who have already crossed over, making you feel comforted and welcomed, as if you're returning to a place you've been before—*which you have!*

As you enter the White Light, you're instantly saturated with a feeling of peace and love. Again, Josiah gives us further explanation:

The White Light is bright and pure; and when you pass through it, you move into a different dimension. The Light is there for a healing purpose, helping you strip away the emotions of your passing—the fear, trauma, pain, and heartache . . . all the hurt. In the White Light, you are healed from the physical pain of dying and are prepared to move on through the next stages of life.

When there is some sort of shock or painful memories upon passing, these are eased when you enter the White Light. A deeper, more complete process of healing occurs when you reach the Afterlife, but passing through the White Light is the first stage of healing, preparing you for what you're about to encounter.

As you can see, there is nothing frightening about passing from this life into the Afterlife. We fear this transition because we don't remember what it was like before we entered our earthly existence. However, as soon as your soul leaves the body, you know instinctively what to do. You've experienced it before—and, just like learning to ride a bike, you never forget it. That knowledge has been locked into your subconscious and becomes available at the time of crossing, so you're completely aware and lose all fear. Furthermore, the soul crosses through the veil and into the White Light in approximately five seconds of earthly time—so it's quick and easy!

Most important to realize is that we've *all* come from the Afterlife, so reentering it is going to feel very familiar. People who are facing the transition and want to leave their earthly life will often say that they want to "go home." Yes, the soul has free will, and each one reacts differently depending on its situation. But everyone—including the most troubled of souls—will be heading toward ultimate healing and growth.

∽

While all souls eventually take the journey of forgiveness and peace in the Afterlife, there are those who break free from their earthly bonds but don't head directly toward the White Light. This is most often because they've chosen to stay behind and attend to unfinished business while still connected closely to the earthly realm. This choice can lead to souls getting stuck between the two worlds and being in need of rescue.

The fate of these so-called ghosts—as well as the troubled or "dark" souls who are denied passage through the White Light—will be explored in the next chapter.

CHAPTER 6

HEAVEN OR HELL— TWO DIFFERENT PATHS

While most souls entering the Afterlife reach the White Light right after passing, others take a different path. Some remain behind so that they can complete unfinished business or because they've become trapped in the vortex between worlds and can't find their way out without help. Others don't get to the pure White Light at all, but must enter first through a different portal that takes them to an alternate healing dimension. The latter are the troubled souls, whose path through the Afterlife is different from most—their fate is referred to in more traditional religions as "hell," the seeming opposite of the White Light's "heaven."

In this chapter I'll cover the passage of both types of souls: those who choose to remain behind for a period of time before transitioning through the White Light; and those who don't go through the pure White Light at all, but arrive in the Afterlife via a different path.

Ghosts and Hauntings

As I've mentioned before, even after a soul is no longer tethered to the body by the silver cord, it still carries with it an individual's personality and experiences. This influences the soul's choices and options as it crosses over . . . and in spite of the many TV shows on the subject, a soul always goes of its own free will. It is never forced, tricked, or manipulated to cross over; it must *want* to leave.

When the soul first leaves the body, there is a sense of newfound freedom: it is free from the restrictions of a body that it may not have liked, free from pain and suffering, and free from other issues that life has put in its path. To get an idea of what this is like, imagine being encased in a full-body cast for a long period of time, then being suddenly released and able to move about without restriction. Multiply that feeling of release by 100, and you'll have some idea of the freedom you'll experience without a body.

Yet not all souls are ready to leave the Earth plane and move on to the White Light. Some believe that they must stay around to help their loved ones grieve, or to assist them in understanding other issues surrounding their transition.

I've encountered some spirits who didn't realize that they had passed away and were continuing to try to live their lives as if they were still here. And very rarely, I've come across a soul who didn't want to cross over due to the fear of what was on the other side or how loved ones might react.

For whatever reason, souls who remain behind—whether by choice or because they're trapped in the vortex between the Earth plane and the Afterlife—are the cause of what's known as a "haunting." You may have experienced a haunting when visiting an old house or medieval castle and sensed a presence in the rooms or halls. That presence can be very real; in fact, it usually indicates that a person who used to live on the premises is reluctant to go, having decided to stay on after leaving his or her body. This type of soul is referred to as a "ghost."

Keep in mind that just feeling a presence does not necessarily mean you've encountered a haunting; rather, you may be sensing the energetic remnants of earlier activity that occurred in that particular location. If you've ever walked around a shopping mall when it has just opened, for instance, you can sense the presence of an energy. That's because thousands of people walk the same pathways in and out of the stores every day, and as they do so, they leave a trail of energy behind them. So what you're picking up on is a kind of "leftover" energy that remains in the space.

In other words, not every creepy feeling you get is a haunting—sometimes you're actually sensing the imprint of energies left by *living* beings. Josiah comments on the difference, explaining that souls who stay behind tend to be troubled, meaning reluctant:

> *Those souls who stay away from the White Light are the troubled ones who cannot move forward. They cannot deal with death and are the ones who are considered to be ghosts that frequent hauntings.*

Ghosts, or reluctant souls, can be helped to cross over into the White Light with the help of the masters and guides on the other side. Spirit guide Ben describes what it's like to work with those souls who have stayed behind:

> *We help them through, showing them the life they can have—the happiness and love that can be achieved—by crossing over into the Afterlife. Some take it; others do not. Some come easily and quickly; others resist. We do what we can. But sometimes it is very tempting for them to remain behind and not cross, especially for those troubled souls who do not want to face their enemies or demons on the other side.*

I've personally had plenty of experience with ghosts and hauntings, and I think the following cases can shed some light on this phenomenon:

— When I was filming my TV show *Life Among the Dead,* we investigated a possible haunting at the Glen Tavern Inn in Santa Paula, California. When the manager, Monica, let me in to Room #307, I almost immediately felt the energy of a woman who was refusing to leave. Monica informed me that an unsolved murder had occurred at the inn some years back. It turns out that I'd encountered the murdered woman's soul, who had remained behind to look for her killer and had been haunting the inn ever since. (Unfortunately, I wasn't able to help this soul move on because she refused to leave, and my night at the inn was spent communicating with many other spirits. In fact, before I knew it, there was someone else who wanted to come in—a man who'd been shot while he'd been gambling in that exact room.)

— I was called in to investigate a home in England owned by a family that was experiencing some strange activity in their children's rooms. Electronic toys were going off in the middle of the night, even though they'd been unplugged and the batteries removed, and lights and TVs were going on and off all by themselves.

My first visit was during the day, and I couldn't pick up on anything. But I knew there was something going on, judging by the anxiety I felt coming from the mother of the house. Being a mother myself, I couldn't ignore this, and knew it meant that *something* had happened. So I went back at about 9 o'clock that evening, and witnessed the strange occurrences for myself.

After some inquiry, I discovered that two children had passed away in a fire at the residence in the early 1940s. The mother had survived but moved away after the tragic accident, probably because she was unable to face being there without her babies. The souls of the children had stayed behind, though—for the past 50 years they'd been searching for their mother so that they could save her from perishing in the fire, too. These lost souls liked to play with toys that belonged to the family now occupying the house, and they were the ones causing the strange disturbances. The "haunted" TV was always found to be tuned to the cartoon station, for instance, so they could entertain themselves as normal kids do.

I had to coax these ghost children to talk to me so that I could begin to guide them through the veil. Communicating with them was difficult because they kept running off to play. Thankfully, my guide Ben stepped in to help, informing me that between the time of the tragedy and the present day, the kids' mother had passed over to the other side. She'd been trying to help her children to come over, but they wouldn't listen. They were having too much fun playing with the current family's toys!

There's always a process of negotiation involved when trying to get a reluctant spirit to cross over, which is why help is often needed. Ben gave me that assistance, showing the children the way to the tunnel and the White Light. Finally, they could see that their mother was waiting for them on the other side. They didn't want to believe it, but after some persuading, they crossed through the veil and into her arms. At last, the house that had been so disturbed by these souls' activities was returned to normal.

— The development of modern technology is helping prove that there is life after death and that souls do exist, sometimes trapped between worlds. To that end, there are many TV shows where people go hunting for ghosts with the use of electromagnetic field (EMF) readers and other electronic devices. Thanks to friends of mine who are part of a West Coast chapter of TAPS (The Atlantic Paranormal Society), I'm familiar with the real-life use of such devices to pick up on disembodied energies or spirits.

My friends shared with me the recording of a spirit talking to someone using one of these devices, and I could clearly hear what it was saying. I was told that the information coming from spirits through these devices is found to be uncannily accurate when researched.

One specific situation that occurred during the Paranormal Society's research involved a "questioner"—a person who asks, "Is anyone there?" and then, "Who are you?"—who was trying to establish the name of the spirit communicating with him in the session. During the 15 or so minutes of pleasantries going back and forth, the questioner continually failed to establish the proper spelling of the spirit's name, to which the spirit condescendingly and quite clearly exclaimed, "You are an idiot!"

Normally, a soul who had crossed over would never say such a rude thing; but a soul who had *not* crossed, and was trapped and still thinking from its earthly form, certainly might. Because such souls can be stubborn, it can be difficult to deal with them—especially since they haven't gone through the White Light and begun their healing journey yet.

Protection from a Psychic Attack

Occasionally, spirits come through who were negative in life, but since they've undergone a process of healing in the Afterlife (which I will explain in more detail in Part III), they're in their highest form when they come to me. Thanks to this healing, all communication with them is as pure and honest as possible.

Others I come into contact with, however, have retained their negativity because they haven't gone through the White Light yet. Whenever I work with these spirits, I have to be sure to protect myself and get help from one of my spirit guides. This ensures my safety and prevents negative energy from becoming attached— otherwise, I could come under psychic attack and have my own energy totally drained.

Have you ever been in a room or a house that was cluttered or overwhelmingly disorganized, and you just didn't feel right? Did you feel tired, low, or sad as you walked away? If so, you may have encountered this kind of attack yourself.

Whenever negative energy is present, it needs to be cleansed psychically. One of the easiest ways to do so is to burn the Native American herb white sage and let the smoke clear a room or some-one's aura. Smudging, as this is known, is an ancient ritual that can cleanse a space of negative spirits. I use this method frequently when I'm in the presence of someone with low or negative energy, or if I have to work in a room that has a heavy feeling about it.

In my first book, *Life Among the Dead,* I discuss one of the most shocking instances of negative energy I've ever experienced. For those of you who haven't read the book, this is what happened.

It was a Friday evening, and I had a girlfriend over to visit. Charlie, who was five at the time, wanted to sleep in Mommy's bed. Since he rarely requested this, I allowed him to do it as a treat for one night.

Around 2 A.M., my friend was getting ready to leave when we heard a loud shriek from Charlie. I ran upstairs to find him sitting bolt upright in bed, staring at a place on the wall above the window. There, a man's shadow was projected, and it looked as if he were wielding a large knife and ready to attack my son.

Charlie was trembling, so I held him tightly as I looked around to see what could have projected the shadow. But by the time I turned back around, the shadow had disappeared, leaving a blank wall with nothing on it. I picked my son up and carried him downstairs, only to find my friend sitting in the living room looking terribly shaken up. She told me that she'd just seen a dark mist come down the stairs, pass right in front of her, and then shoot out toward the kitchen.

I decided to leave that evening and return the next day to deal with whatever it was in the light of day. I knew I could handle it and wasn't afraid, but I didn't want Charlie to be in the house. He is a sensitive child and had already been traumatized enough by that dark and sinister energy.

The following day, I returned home to give a few readings, leaving Charlie with my parents so that I could tackle and confront this lurking spirit myself. My experience told me that this soul wasn't going to leave unless I allowed it to communicate with me. (This is often the case with spirits who stay behind—they want to get a message across, so they hang around and cause mischief until that message is delivered.)

Sure enough, the spirit returned. I sensed its arrival while sitting in meditation in the room I gave my readings in. I moved upstairs to the bedroom where the activity had started, and began communicating with the spirit. He told me that his name was Jimmy, and that he'd abused the three young daughters of the woman he married. He proceeded to give me the names of the girls.

I asked him why he'd scared the life out of my son. He said that he only knew how to get the attention of children, but he had to use whatever he could to get to me. Although his reasoning made sense, I wasn't happy when I heard it, thinking, *Oh great, use my son!*

Jimmy went on to tell me that he'd committed suicide, and that he didn't want to cross over because he was afraid of meeting his parents for fear of how they would react. It turns out that his parents had abused *him,* just as he'd done to his stepdaughters. He feared that if he crossed over, he might become trapped with them in the spirit world and it would be a bad situation.

Jimmy wanted to be healed of his fear, but he remained a deeply troubled soul that needed to move to the White Light for any healing to take place. After some coaxing on my part, and with the help of Ben and other guides, he eventually did just that— he crossed over into the White Light and into the arms of his protector, a spirit guide who in life had intervened to keep him away from his abusers.

This soul had come to me in the hopes that I could tell his family he was sorry for abusing the daughters and for the way he'd died. It was comforting to know that he was now safe and being healed by Spirit, but it was also a lesson for me in that I learned that there are some souls who stay behind because they fear being confronted by their past deeds.

Unfinished Business

Souls who stay behind to take care of unfinished business inhabit the vortex, or the space between worlds. Imagine two panes of glass, with the earthly world being one pane and the spirit world being the other. The space between the glass would be the vortex, where spirits get a toehold and are able to stay. In this way, departed souls share the world and are able to make contact with us.

Souls are not restricted to staying in the vortex, never passing into the White Light—they can choose to stay or choose to leave. But if they stay a long time, they become trapped, unable to move on until their business is finished. An example of unfinished business is when a murder takes place, and the soul of the victim knows who did it and stays on to help family members collect the evidence.

When souls are in the vortex, they can reveal themselves in pronounced ways, sometimes by placing clues in an earthly person's way and influencing physical objects in order to manifest the help they need. This generally occurs only in extreme cases, though; most souls get across their needs or the information they want to provide in a loving and gentle way.

This was the case for a soul who came through during a show I was doing a few years ago on the East Coast. Dave was trapped in the vortex because he'd been murdered, and his killer had not yet been found. He wanted to communicate with a person in the audience, but I didn't know who it was. So I just called out the name "Dave," and his daughter responded in surprise. She hadn't expected her father to contact her—perhaps because his tragic death had only happened a few weeks before.

Spirits who haven't crossed through the veil yet can come through very strongly, mostly because they haven't shaken off their earthly ties. But they can also be very strong because they're using all the energy around them to communicate. That's why I often find that when I'm working, the energy is quickly drained from batteries around me, causing devices to cut out in minutes when they should last at least five hours. It's a hazard of my work, and I always have to have standby batteries in my microphone for this situation.

Dave's presence was very strong, and he showed me that that he was in the vortex between worlds. Technically, he wasn't trapped—he'd chosen to stay to help with his murder investigation, intending to cross over once it was solved. I spoke with his daughter in the audience, giving the details he provided that could help solve the crime. She listened to the names and dates I gave her, but she responded that she had no idea what I was talking about. This is not an uncommon occurrence when I help people solve mysteries such as a murder, so I always ask them to do their homework and research the meaning of the message.

Still in shock over her father's murder, Dave's daughter was not in a fit state to remember all the information I'd given her. She barely took anything in; fortunately, a kind woman sitting next to her wrote down detailed notes and gave them to her, recording facts and names to check in order to further aid the investigation.

About three weeks later, I was contacted by a private investigator who was working to solve Dave's murder. He'd discovered some information that he hadn't shared with the family because he wasn't sure if it was true. He was trying to gather evidence when Dave's daughter handed him the notes from my reading. He told me that the information in the notes had matched the details he'd discovered, confirming that he'd pinpointed the actual person who had murdered Dave. What was in the notes gave him further assistance in finding the evidence he needed. When I gave the information to Dave's daughter, I had no idea what it meant. I don't process what I receive or try to understand it—I simply convey it as if it's a direct translation.

Using the information I'd provided during the reading, the private investigator was ultimately able to gather enough evidence to lead to a conviction of Dave's murderer. I didn't know of this outcome until I received an e-mail telling me what had happened and thanking me for my part in it. As I read the message, I remember feeling a familiar spirit around me. It was Dave, showing me that he'd crossed over and was now in the White Light. He could continue his journey in the Afterlife, knowing that his family and friends were safe from harm.

The Rescue Mission

Sometimes souls in the vortex cannot make it to the White Light on their own and need rescuing. I typically do this work in my sleep, astral-traveling to other dimensions to help souls who need some aid in crossing over. I've done this for years . . . but before I knew I did it, I used to wonder why I woke up from a long sleep totally exhausted when I should have felt refreshed.

During my meditation one day, Ben told me that I am a connection between some lost souls and the Earth realm. He said that those souls seek me out because they need help conveying a message to their loved ones. Once I've assisted them in this process, the souls are able to move on.

At the end of the meditation, I asked Ben if I'd be permitted to remember what happened on one of my journeys. I'm sure he thought I was doubting what he told me about rescuing lost souls—and in a way, I suppose I was. But I was also curious and wanted to remember what had happened during one of these "rescue missions." Thankfully, I was given the chance to do so.

One morning upon waking up, I recalled leaving my body during the night and kissing Charlie on the cheek as I left. When I met up with Ben, he joked that I always checked up on Charlie before I left my body to undertake a mission. The next thing I knew, I'd crossed some water and was standing next to a soul who was bent down with his head in his hands, crying in front of his wife and child.

"Are you dead, too?" he asked when he saw me.

"No," I answered, "but I can help you get a message to your wife."

The man told me he wanted his wife to understand that he'd unintentionally taken an overdose of drugs and hadn't committed suicide. He explained how he'd suffered from depression and severe headaches, which had prompted his physician to prescribe a combination of drugs for him. One night he took his medication for depression, but because he was suffering from headaches as well, he also took a painkiller before falling asleep. In the middle of the night, he woke up with a dull throbbing in his head, so he took more medicine—forgetting that he'd already taken some. As a result, he overdosed on his prescribed drugs. His family and friends thought that he'd purposely overdosed due to a history of depression, but that was not the case.

The man wanted to show those he cared for what had actually happened. So with my help, and the assistance of other guides and helpers, he was able to connect with his wife and travel with her astrally so that she could see exactly what had happened. During this journey, they shared a beautiful, loving time together. After he left her, he was guided onward toward the White Light, stopping briefly to embrace me and say thank you. I left as his wife was starting to wake up.

About a year later, I was holding an event when a woman approached me and said, "Lisa, you came to me in a dream about a year ago and brought my husband to me." This was not unusual, as many people tell me that I pop into their dreams to help them or teach them about spirituality.

But then she added, "You helped my husband show me that he hadn't committed suicide, but it was actually an accidental overdose that caused his death. He didn't mean to do it, and he wanted me to know he loved me."

The woman started to describe the surroundings of our dream meeting, which were strangely familiar to me until I realized that her husband was the person I remembered traveling with on my rescue mission. I later got confirmation of my feelings when Ben appeared with his arms crossed, smirking and nodding as I exclaimed, "Wow—you're not kidding me—that really was the person! I remember!" It was as if Ben was mocking me for doubting him, telling me, *I told you so!*

The Dark Side

Next, I want to explore why some souls don't pass through the White Light, but instead take another entryway to the Afterlife. Due to their actions on Earth, these are the dark souls, those who have committed terrible acts—the true sociopaths, serial killers, and mass murderers. I feel that it's important to mention these souls when looking at the whole process of passing. Since we've covered the soul's passage to the White Light, it's only fair to consider the other side of the coin. *Where there is light, there has to be dark.*

I was very fortunate to have a lengthy channeling session on this subject with Ben and Josiah the Elder. They helped me understand what the dark side of a soul's passage is like and where such troubled souls go. It's certainly not a place *I* would like to visit, but I do know that it exists. This is how Ben explains it:

> *Darker souls who have not yet passed tend to gather together, so you get areas where they congregate to produce the most dramatic hauntings. It is nothing to worry about, and there is*

little that can be done. We have teams of helpers on this side to assist them, but getting them to move on is not always possible. We do our best to protect others.

At the time of transition, some souls choose to turn away from the White Light so they will not have to face their own demons in the earthly life, demons they will not want to look at or deal with. Many have destroyed the life force within others. While they can never destroy the soul, as a result of their actions, the soul can become hidden. You can see a hidden soul in the hollow, vacant eyes of a person, reflecting that the soul is still there, but it is lost and needs to be found. Smiling eyes can tell a lot, but eyes that are hollow tell the whole story.

What Ben is saying here is that when some souls start their transition through the veil, they decide not to cross over because they fear that in the Afterlife, they'll have to deal with how they tried to destroy their own or someone else's soul.

We can all relate to some degree of having "hidden" our soul, something we do to avoid becoming hurt through rejection or disappointment. We can see it in some people's eyes, especially in photographs—they may be smiling at the camera, but their eyes are dead. If we look at earlier photos of those same individuals, we might see the shine and the sparkle back in their eyes, indicating a time when they had not yet buried their soul.

You don't have to be psychic to pick up something like this; it's visual and very apparent to everyone. It's true what they say about the eyes being the windows to the soul, and when the soul has become obscured, it no longer shines through for all to see.

Josiah's words explain further what happens during the passage of dark souls:

Not everyone who passes and starts out to cross the veil goes through the pure White Light. Those who have done wrong go through a different light to another place in the Afterlife. Their light is white, but it is not pure. It will take them to a place of healing, but they will not mix with those of a higher spirit. They will only mix with those of a similar energy—those they have been with before in earthly existence—until they have healed from their wrongdoings and come back and learned their lessons.

At the time of their exit, dark souls take a pathway that is different from other souls. They go through the veil to another light and another healing dimension in the Afterlife. There are many levels in the spirit world, and each one is specific to the soul's healing journey. Dark souls at this juncture have no choice about where to go, unless they decide to stay earthbound—this is a choice some make and, as we have seen, results in hauntings.

Many on Earth call this alternate path "hell," but the hell we imagine based on the Bible and other traditions is not accurate. In fact, there is no hell as we might imagine it; hell is a state of mind rather than a real place. It's up to us to change this view—we have the free will to grow and come to a new state of mind, and we can do so with the help of our guides and helpers in the Afterlife.

As Josiah states:

Dark souls do come back to the Earth plane, and they need to. The consciousness of their own mind has put them in the place they call hell. There is no hell; it is a state of mind. They have to go through the same process every soul goes through to allow themselves to heal and move forward and grow. So even though they return, it does not happen right away. They must do the healing work more thoroughly, or we would constantly be seeing souls as dark as Hitler returning, and that would not be a good thing.

Those souls who have committed great wrongs will go toward a different light, accompanied by other souls who are similar to them so that they do not taint the souls that have crossed to the White Light.

Josiah explains what happens when a dark soul passes:

They are given a guardian, a spirit helper who follows them closely. I suppose the only thing in your world that resembles their path is a prison, but in the Afterlife, they are given support to integrate back into the world after their "term." They are carefully guided and know that they are being watched at all times.

Some of these souls pass at a young age because they got into dangerous situations due to their risky behavior. They are given to parents who are strong enough to cope with their upbringing, as they will often be in trouble at a young age. But be clear that not every child who passes is in this category. There are many reasons why souls pass young.

Throughout my meditations, I was shown how souls who have created serious problems for themselves and others go through a healing process in this alternate dimension in the Afterlife. Part of their fate is to return back to earthly existence more quickly than other souls do—but unlike other souls, they're denied a choice of when to return and which parents to return to. The masters of the Afterlife decide their pathway, assigning to them the best circumstances to help them move forward and continue to be healed.

In a channeling received from Josiah, further light is shed on what happens to the dark souls among us:

Sometimes these dark souls can be straightened out within a few lifetimes. Lifetimes for us are like days for you, so although you may feel it is a long time, in retrospect, it is not. For everyone, there will be many lives and many opportunities.

Back in earthly existence, these returning souls are given spirit guides to help them meet the people they have to associate with in order to acquire the lessons they need to learn. Somewhere on Earth, they will interact with a person who will change their lives and help them see that they have been making the wrong moves. This may happen when they find God through religion, thereby gaining peace and comfort from being with the "chosen" people to help them on their journey.

You have noticed how like attracts like—the energy of a person attracts similar energy. When dark souls reincarnate, they are often put together with others who are the same, or they naturally congregate with others of that energy. But only if they alter their paths through their own free will, will they ever see the pure White Light and be able to move on to the next process in their journey.

For example, a soul who has been placed on this Earth plane to help, nurture, and love others may then cross paths with these dark souls. Such loving souls are the chosen ones whose purpose is to change how people view life and show them the light from the Earth plane. These souls often have jobs of the highest spiritual calling.

They often stand out as the strongest willed of people, and their faith and love do not waver. However, if a situation does get too much for them to handle, they walk away before the light fades in their own soul. Otherwise, they are placed on a higher spiritual path to remind them that the light is behind them.

Often, those dark souls who have come back will continue to hold on to the anger they have carried with them through their many incarnations. This is the great Circle of Life, eventually resulting in a balance of karma and moving them on to the White Light. Through the guidance and the love we give them, and through the people we send to help them, they will find the joy they deserve and need.

Many people think of those who suffer from mental illnesses as dark and troubled souls. This is not the case; dark souls are those who have *intentionally* inflicted harm on other people, not those who are suffering from an illness. But Ben brings up a good point:

People who have suffered from mental illness go straight to the White Light and begin their healing process. It is surprising to us how many people on the Earth plane who do not value the lives of others are placed in the same class as the mentally ill.

In life, our legal system sometimes finds those who have done great harm to others to be mentally ill, and thus not responsible for their actions. (Of course, this may be true in some cases.) When mentally ill people cross over, they go straight to the pure White

Light—but those who have made the choice to harm others and have not suffered any kind of mental illness are denied that path and must find their healing via an alternate route.

Suicide and the Soul's Path

When a suicide occurs, those left behind often find themselves asking some disturbing questions: *Could I have done something? How could I have helped? Did he really do this, or did something else happen? What drove her to take her own life?* Many of these questions remain unanswered, making it very hard on those who are grieving. For some who never get any answers, it can become difficult to move on in life.

Suicides are tragic events, but the soul of a person who commits suicide does not share the same path as a dark soul who must cross into an alternate healing dimension. The path of this soul is to go toward the pure White Light on his or her journey of healing in the Afterlife.

However, those who have committed a murder and then committed suicide will travel to the other dimension and not go through the pure White Light, unless they decide that they don't want to cross and choose to remain behind. They have taken someone else's life in addition to their own; therefore, they must go through the process in the Afterlife we've just discussed, and then return back to earthly existence to grow through learning their lessons.

Ben makes it very clear:

> *Not all suicides go to the White Light. We have to remember that suicides can cause a great deal of distress and anger. These are normal reactions, but they often arise because the person passing intended such harm. Also, when people take their own life, they back out of the contract made between their higher being and themselves. They have not finished the journey. The path they set out to complete is broken, and this has to be resolved.*

Some suicides are part of a murder-suicide situation, brought about intentionally. Those souls will have to return and relive a life in the world again, but first they will go through the darker side, as they have taken someone else's life. There is little that we spirit guides can do on this front; we have to believe that we are doing all we can. If they choose not to pass through into the darker side and not return for further lessons, then they will remain in between, haunting the places where they lived previously and never finding a resolution.

There is more information pertaining to suicides, and I am going to use the channeled messages from Josiah and Ben to explain this process. First up is Josiah:

Suicides need extra support and are given an immense amount of help as they travel through the process. They may have to work harder to look at their lives, but they understand that it is necessary to get their particular lessons. In some cases, it has been preprogrammed for those souls to take their own lives, providing lessons that both parents and entire families may need to learn. People may not like it, but they sometimes need the experience of a suicide to heal. You see, we put people together in families for a reason. Some were placed to heal past wounds; others to help another move on. Often a passing can help two people in a family pull together and overcome certain issues. It is uncomplicated to us, but difficult for us to explain.

And now, here's Ben:

Suicides happen because people have decided to drop out of life. Of course, those individuals will have to come back, because their soul needs to be healed and taken back to the Source for guidance, comfort, and understanding. However, this pathway has already been predestined before they came to the Earth plane. We have guides on this side to help with this process, healers who are knowledgeable in the natural pathways for finding resolution for the soul. These healers are very pow-erful, and they frequently attend temples where they perform daily practices to help others in moving forward with their life.

There is no real-time element for this process that we can determine. Souls come and heal, and then move on when they need to. It is not easy; it is very challenging work. But once the soul has discovered its way and becomes stronger, it is ready again for the lifetime ahead.

I find it comforting to know that when people pass from sui-cide, their souls are guided and helped along by powerful healers who help them look at their lives and then assist them in return-ing to life. We all have a choice in determining the life we return to (which I'll discuss in a later chapter), but those who have taken their own earthly lives will have fewer options because there are specific lessons to be learned. Souls are advised by their guides as to what would be the right family to help them with those lessons.

During one of my channeled meditations, Josiah gave me a piece of astounding personal information, which is relevant to this topic. I share it here because it shows how a soul who committed suicide can come back with a totally new outlook on life:

Sometimes those who commit suicide are very brave souls who sacrifice their lives for others to be happy. You actually did that in a past life when you brought about your own death in order to enable your wife to move on (you were a man in that lifetime). You knew you could not be with her and that she needed and wanted to be with someone else, but you were part of a religious group that would not allow you to divorce or move out of that relationship. You had no choice. You were both miserable, so you poisoned yourself with food, which is why you are so wary about what you eat in this lifetime. There was suspicion that she killed you, but you had decided to kill yourself, and you wrote a letter to your parents confirming this.

Further, it was revealed that your wife had been cheating on you with a close friend. It was terribly hurtful, but you decided that you loved her enough to leave this life. You spent a while in the Afterlife looking at this incarnation, and then you vowed to return with a fresh, new pair of eyes. You decided to help others see the light and enjoy all the riches that life can offer. Most important, you accomplished your goal of teaching others what life is like on the other side.

Your goal and purpose in this lifetime is to teach. You will be teaching others in their spiritual development for many, many years. To do so, you must stay grounded. We cannot tell you how to accomplish this because your own actions—your karma—determine how you will move on in life. You have to grow, and you will. You already have beyond your years, so stay true to who you are. Your dreams and goals were set long before your current lifetime and know no bounds of time.

From my story, you can see that with help and guidance, a person who has left earthly existence through a suicide can reincarnate with a new view of life and continue his or her journey of growth, and even service. I do know that I have lived other lives since this one, many of which have helped me both to develop spiritually and to acquire the information and wisdom I'm sharing with you now.

∽

For those who pass through the pure White Light, a great healing adventure awaits. But before those souls are permitted to begin their healing journey in the Afterlife, they meet up with the spirits who have been guiding them in life—and who will continue to accompany them along the way.

⌘

CHAPTER 7

SOUL CONNECTIONS

After you pass, but before you can begin your journey of healing and growth on the other side (a process I thoroughly cover in Part III), you must spend time in an area that is the threshold to the Afterlife, referred to as the Meeting Room. Here, you'll be greeted by people you knew in this lifetime but who have passed on, such as your parents, grandparents, or other relatives. In Josiah's words:

> *Once your soul is through the White Light, it is met and greeted by loved ones, guides, and others who have assisted you through your journey. They are the ones who have helped you all along, and they are here to help you now.*

Josiah is also referring here to your "soul connections." These include your team of spirit guides, your soul mate, and your soul family—those who have been with you during your lifetime and will accompany you on your journey to come. This chapter will fill you in on the details of these souls who are so important in your life . . . and your life after life.

What Are Spirit Guides?

During your time on Earth, you are supported by guidance from Spirit in the form of your guides. These are souls you have known before, possibly in your past lives or your previous times in the Afterlife. Before you became earthbound in your current life, you made a contract with these souls for them to become your spirit guides. To perform this service, they chose to remain behind in the Afterlife while you incarnated. This is possibly because you assisted them in a past life, and they want to return the favor this time around.

The purpose of spirit guides is to help you on the Earth plane and through the passage to the other side, fulfilling the pact you made with them before you incarnated. As you live your life, they provide invaluable support to you. Even though you might not even be aware of them, they are always watching out for you.

Some spirit guides appear in your life at specific times to help you when needed. But others are with you the whole time, coming on at birth and staying with you steadily over the duration of your lifetime. One of these is your "master spirit guide," who heads up the team of other guides and directs or invites their participation in your process. You've already met my master guide, Ben. Even though I was an adult when my grandmother first introduced him to me, he has been with me since birth and has watched over my every step of growth and learning.

Yet whether they're with you all the time or for a brief period, the job of each and every one of your guides is to help you learn as many lessons as you can while on the Earth plane—and that requires them to be a team of helpers, operating in multiple ways.

In their capacity as helpers, your spirit guides talk to you all the time. The words they use may sound very much like your own, as if you're talking to yourself; however, if you listen carefully, you'll notice a slight tone change when they speak. Using a piano keyboard as an analogy, imagine that your own voice is in the key of C. Your guides talk to you in the key of C-sharp, half a tone higher than the pitch of your own voice. This is subtle, but once you've made the distinction, you can always tell if it is your own voice or that of your guides speaking to you.

Your spirit guides also communicate with you via your gut feelings or intuition. You may get their messages via an inner voice, such as when you say to yourself, *I'm not sure I should do that.* Yet how many times have you been in a situation in which you knew you shouldn't do something, but you went ahead and did it anyway? You may have assumed that the inner voice telling you not to do it was only your mind playing tricks on you, but it wasn't!

Our guides cannot run our lives or dictate what we should do—we still have free will and must make our own decisions, as they are not allowed to make them for us. I can recall many times when I went against my own initial gut feeling, only to discover that I should have listened more closely and not ignored what turned out to be the voice and influence of my spirit guide.

We all make choices that we regret—it's part of life and our continual learning. But whether we pay attention or not to those inner voices, our spirit guides will continue to communicate with us and try to influence events in our life, making sure that we have the experiences we need to fulfill the contract we set before our birth. They won't give up because we don't listen . . . in fact, their attempts can sometimes be quite dramatic, as you'll see in this example from my own life.

The first time I came to America on an extended vacation, I was preparing to return to England when I became very ill and had to go to the hospital—resulting in the NDE I told you about earlier. I didn't know it at the time, but my spirit guides were setting it up for me to meet TV legend Merv Griffin, who later became the executive producer of my show *Lisa Williams: Life Among the Dead*. I never would have met him if I'd gone back to the U.K. as scheduled.

Although I'd had surgery, I was doing fine. However, the doctors felt that it was unsafe for me to be in a pressurized cabin on such a long flight, so they ordered me to stay in L.A. for another ten days of recovery. During those ten days, "circumstances" came together for me to meet Merv. That meeting changed my life, giving me a chance to develop as a medium, and putting me on a path to fulfill my purpose as a teacher. (Nan Frances had told me that it would be an older man who'd bring me to America and put me in front of thousands of people: little did I know it would happen the way it did!)

✺

Spirit guides can bring about many wonderful events in your life, leading to your spiritual fulfillment and evolution, but there are times when what happens isn't so wonderful. I was once asked, "If we all have spirit guides, then how come there are so many evil people in the world doing terrible things?" This is a very valid question, and the answer tells us much about the human/spirit relationship.

When I asked Ben about this, he channeled the following response:

> *Understand that we guides can only show you the pathway—we cannot make you walk it. It is up to you which way you decide to go and how you want to live your life. We help you heal the scars and wounds from past lives so that you can become a highly evolved soul, but these experiences are your lessons. We can facilitate your evolvement, but we cannot make your choices for you. So when people do terrible, evil things, it is their choice—made in the freedom of their soul—to take what pathway they will take. We can only lead them from there.*

I found myself wondering, *Do some people ever get a bad spirit guide?* Since Ben can hear my thoughts and feel my feelings, and he knows me better than I know myself, it was no surprise to hear him say:

> *No spirit guide is "bad." We are always acting to fulfill a soul's purpose, to ensure that it makes the most out of the life it has. So even an evil person cannot have a bad spirit guide.*
>
> *Be assured that a spirit guide will never give up on you, no matter how "wrong" your choices may be. We will work with you until the day you transition, so we will continue to help straighten out any pathway you take.*

From this I hope it is clear that the role of your spirit guide is to look out for you, and to ensure that you are safe and protected until you've fulfilled your purpose in this lifetime. How that may look is not always easy to understand, and you have the free will to not follow your guides' influence and make mistakes in life. Yet you will always receive the guidance you need to meet the conditions of your contract, and that guidance will be given freely with love, regardless of your choices.

Your Other Guides

As I mentioned before, some of your soul connections are spirits who visited you in life, but only on a temporary basis—they arrived for a specific assignment to assist you and then left when they were done.

For example, one of my guides is a female energy named Lucinda who pops in and out as I need her. She's very important when I'm teaching or doing readings for large audiences at my live shows. At times she takes over for Ben, who normally acts as the "gatekeeper" to get communicating spirits in line. But unlike Ben, who only lets in one spirit at a time, Lucinda opens the gate for few spirits at a time. This can be frustrating for me, since I can't always tell who I'm talking to, but it's also a fun challenge.

Lucinda is very strong when I teach, giving me information when I'm planning my lessons, as well as during the actual teaching process. I know when she's with me because her energy mixes with my own, making a noticeable ripple in my aura. It's not always easy for an untrained person to recognize being visited by an impromptu spirit guide—but if you teach yourself to be sensitive to energy, you can notice a different vibration around you, even though you may not be able to say exactly what it is.

Sometimes the messages and communications coming directly from these guides can be difficult to receive accurately. I can tell when I'm working with a guide other than Ben because I have to work harder to get the message that's coming through, which is not the norm for me. It's much like the way you may have to adapt to different people in different situations, saying a variety of things in order to get your point across. That's what a guide who is attempting to contact someone must do, and it can take a lot of effort on the part of the person receiving the message to get that message clearly.

Keep in mind that when you arrive in the Meeting Room, your *full team* of spirit guides will be waiting for you; you'll have a chance to greet all of those who have helped you through tough situations, such as career adjustments, relationship changes, and the general ups and downs of life.

Some of the spirits you meet may not have helped you through your earthly life at all, but are waiting to be your guides through the healing process you are about to embark upon in the Afterlife. Of this category of soul connections, Josiah further enlightens us:

> *They have all been assigned a particular job: to help you heal, particularly from any pain; to help you look at your life; to guide you through the Afterlife until you get on your feet; to help you deal with the emotions that you left; and to help you deal with your loved ones' emotions, which might still be with you. As you have seen, more than one guide will be there to help you connect. They all have a purpose, something that they will be doing to focus on helping you through your process in the Afterlife, and they will all be waiting for you when you first arrive.*

Meeting Your Soul Mate

Josiah reveals another soul connection that will be waiting for you when you arrive at the threshold of the Afterlife:

> *Your soul mate will also be there to greet you; if your soul mate has not yet arrived, because he or she is still in earthly existence, then you will be prepared for his or her arrival. However, you may not have known your soul mate in this life, having made a pact together before your birth to take turns and alternate roles, one helping the other as the other has done.*

A soul mate—sometimes called a "twin flame"—is a spirit who perfectly complements you as if he or she is your other half. It's possible that your soul mate is also your master spirit guide, and that you made a pact before birth that one of you would stay behind and help the other through his or her lessons in life.

When you meet your soul mate in the Meeting Room, you will experience a completeness unlike anything you have ever imagined. The feeling is one of being totally whole, lacking nothing. Emotions are intensified, reaching heights you never knew in your earthly body. Furthermore, you won't have the self-esteem issues you may have had in life, because those personal concerns are diminished and even cleared away as you embark upon your healing process in the Afterlife.

As Josiah has channeled, you may or may not have met your soul mate as a person in life—it might not be the individual you were married to or had a relationship with, even though you and your earthly partner loved each other very much. You and your soul mate may have decided not to meet up with each other on Earth because you both felt that you had work to do and had to be free to touch others' lives without any distractions. If you were together, you'd be completely wrapped up in each other, sharing the love and healing that is part of the soul-mate relationship. Included in your pact is the agreement to return back to each other in the Afterlife.

If you're fortunate enough to meet your soul mate in this life, you may find that he or she comes to you later on rather than when you're young. That's because you need to first experience many lessons with other people. When you do meet your soul mate, you'll find that the normal sensation of being in love intensifies, especially if you're someone who easily senses energy and picks up on emotions.

Sometimes it's overwhelming because you almost instantly know that you'll be with this person forever, often within the first few minutes of meeting him or her. Such intimacy might frighten the two of you, since you may have been molded by your upbringing to not express your feelings. It can also be a jolt if you discover that your soul mate is the same sex as you, but you've always had relationships with people of the opposite sex. If you're a woman, for example, you might wonder, *If this person is my soul mate, then why isn't she a man?* But remember, these arrangements were made through a contract before birth, so a same-sex relationship could very well be part of a lesson that you and your soul mate—as well as your families—needed to learn.

The story of my client Ann perfectly illustrates this. I read for her for many years, during which she was happily married with two children. She loved her life, her kids, and her husband, and greatly enjoyed her job. And then one day, Julie started to work at Ann's office. My client got to know her and felt an instant connection, as if she'd known this woman before. Ann was very intuitive and so was Julie, a commonality they discussed when they got together over drinks.

Neither of them could figure out why they felt so close, so fast. To me, Ann described their connection as overwhelmingly powerful. As time passed, things intensified, going from a work relationship to a more personal and intimate one. Although Julie was gay, Ann had never been with a woman before and was confused by her feelings.

Immediately, I told her, "You have met your soul mate." She was astounded and then asked me if I was talking about her husband.

I didn't know what to say at first, but as ever, I was totally honest. "No," I replied, "although you love your husband, the person who is your soul mate couldn't give you the children that you so desperately wanted, so she had to come to you later on in your life."

At that point, Ann broke down in tears. She said that Julie had gone away on business, and she felt as if her soul had been torn and part of her was missing. My client couldn't function in the way she normally did, and she didn't know what to do. On the one hand, she didn't want to break up her immediate family; on the other, she knew that she couldn't live without this woman. Ann also had the added pressure of worrying about her parents and extended family, all of whom had very strong opinions about same-sex relationships.

Over a period of time, my client took the steps to sort out her feelings and rearrange her life. She eventually divorced her husband, and the children came to live with her and Julie. Today, Ann and her ex-husband still have a close relationship, and he has come to adore Julie. We discovered in my readings that he was part of Ann's "soul family" connection—a group I will describe shortly—as were their children. But the two of them were not destined to stay together in this lifetime. (This man is now happily remarried.)

Parting from her husband was the easy part—telling her parents was much more difficult. Ann's mother and father took the news that she was in a same-sex relationship very hard and actually refused to speak to her. Eventually, they came to see the love that was between the two women and grew to accept the idea, although they didn't like it. This was a lesson for everyone in the family, including Ann herself, in allowing others who may differ from them to have their own life.

Ann recently told me that her family is very close now, and she is grateful for this and the guidance that her spirit guides gave her when coming through in the many readings she's done with me. She said she'd learned that when we fall in love, it is with the soul of a person, not the gender. I believe that this is true—our soul mates can come to us in many ways, shapes, and forms, and none may be as we expect.

∾

When you meet your soul mate in this life, the feeling you both experience can be unbearable at times. You always feel connected and constantly want to be together, finding it hard to focus on tasks that you're normally able to do. This is more than an infatuation; it is an emotion that fills your heart. When you're together, you feel complete; when you're miles apart, it feels like a piece of you is missing. And when discussing your dreams together, you and your soul mate may discover that you've had the exact same dream—because you've astral-traveled together.

You may not be able to express the love you have for each other easily, finding the words *I love you* inadequate to convey the intensity of what you feel for one another. The whole thing is very emotional for you both, and initially you might not understand it. You may question why you're feeling certain emotions you've never felt before, even though you've had other partners in your life.

It might not always be an easy relationship when you connect with your soul mate, however; often he or she is very much the opposite of you in personality, temperament, and even life goals and directions. Know that it's natural for each of you to have different tastes and opinions, because you may have come from very different backgrounds and were molded to a certain way of thinking, but you will appreciate each other's lives immensely. Also, your soul mate is meant to balance you, providing what you've been missing in life. This can be a fulfilling but also rocky path, requiring you to overcome many obstacles that cause conflicts and disruptions.

I know from personal experience that many of us who are healers and lightworkers struggle to find the right love relationships on the Earth plane, as we've devoted our lives to others. Of course, our struggles stem from the lessons we must learn.

Any highly evolved soul who's on the planet to teach and help others spiritually needs a partner who will provide a balance. This partner may also be a highly evolved and spiritual soul; if that is the case, there must be some grounding elements in the couple's relationship, or they'd both find it difficult to be present in their lives. For example, one partner could devote him- or herself to spirituality, using those gifts to heal others; while the other could be involved in a grounding career, such as a lawyer or something within the corporate world, reserving spirituality for his or her personal life. Being a lawyer can provide someone with opportunities to learn many things through interacting with a variety of people, while also helping that person keep his or her feet on the ground.

Your Soul Family

In addition to spirit guides and soul mates, you have connections with kindred spirits—your soul family. These are souls with whom you're meant to be grouped in life because you can collectively touch people's lives and help them. This may not be the same family you lived with or were associated with on the Earth plane, however. Who these individuals are depends on what your lessons are and what your contract dictated before you returned to embodiment on Earth.

When you meet members of your soul family on the other side, you'll instantly feel that you know them—and that you have known them all your life. If you think about all of your friends, relatives, co-workers, and acquaintances, you'll immediately know those who are part of your soul family and who have impacted your life on such a level. Some of them may have gone in and out of your earthly life, but you will always be connected.

Much like your relationship with your soul mate, your connection with your soul-family members on the Earth plane can be intense. Even though you may be miles apart, you're able to pick up on their feelings, sensing when they're going to call or e-mail you. You can say that you truly love them, and they love and understand you equally. For instance, I have connections with several people in my life who are members of my soul family, including my best friend. Even though we live on opposite sides of the planet at this time, we always feel as if we are right next door to each other.

Know that once you get to the Afterlife, you're going to once again meet these souls who love you and only have your best interests at heart. You'll return to your soul family—the family that loves you unconditionally, helps you grow spiritually, and remains with you throughout your time in the Afterlife.

As you can see, your soul family, soul mate, and spirit guides all form a remarkable group that is devoted to you and committed to your growth and development as a soul—not only in life, but also on your continuing journey in the Afterlife.

The next chapter was inspired by a conversation I had with Josiah the Elder about the process of rebirth we all go through during our journey in the Afterlife. Life and death, death and life—the two complement each other when it comes to our overall evolution as souls. Understanding how our process is one of rebirth into a greater life, starting with the welcome home from all those who await us on the threshold of the Afterlife, is my next topic.

CHAPTER 8

LIFE ENABLED BY DEATH—REBIRTH!

Spirits on the other side view death very differently than we do. Where we see an ending to life, they perceive an opportunity for the soul to move on to the next stages of existence in the Afterlife—a rebirth.

I understand that the use of the term *rebirth* when talking about death may seem like a contradiction, as I initially had the same reaction. You see, during the course of writing this book, I received a channeling from Josiah in which he spoke of life being *enabled by death*. I questioned him about this strange phrase, not sure why he was referring to the experience of the Afterlife in this way. Here is an excerpt from that conversation, beginning with the subject he'd been addressing in the channeling:

> JOSIAH: *In the White Light, you are healed from the physical pain of dying and are prepared to move on through the next stages of <u>life.</u>*
> LISA: Life?
> JOSIAH: *Yes, my dear, <u>life</u>—as life is enabled by death.*

A Revealing Message

Sometime after I received Josiah's perplexing statement, I came to understand what he meant. I was doing a reading for my client Cathy, whose son had recently passed, and what I received revealed how death can indeed be a rebirth.

But before we get to a transcript of Cathy's reading, I want to share how messages from Spirit are delivered directly through me, usually without any interpretation on my part.

When I act as a medium receiving messages from Spirit, it is frequently not as straightforward as one might think. As I've mentioned, spirits lack a mouth to pronounce words as we would, so their voices sound muffled to me. Imagine that someone is speaking through a tight scarf wrapped around his or her mouth—that's very similar to what I hear.

Because of this "handicap," spirits have to find other ways to get messages across to me, and this is often done symbolically. They might send messages through thought projection, occasionally placing words in my head. Sometimes the words don't make up a whole sentence; from them, I may get a feeling or emotion, perhaps the emotion of love, which is normally located in my stomach area.

The spirit could also show me something more concrete, such as someone's initials. If I ask for more information, I might see a visual symbol, maybe something like a heart or other familiar icon. My job is to communicate these clues to the person I'm reading for so that he or she can relate to them, and then I help pull it all together into a meaningful message.

Once, as I read for a woman whose husband had passed, I received the following information: the words *walk, tree,* and *cold;* someone's initials; and the symbol of a heart. In the following transcript of that reading, you can see how we worked with what I was given to arrive at a powerful message for my client:

LISA: Your husband is showing me a *heart.* It's as though you went for a *walk* on a *cold* day together, and you decided to carve your initials into a *tree* and surround them with a heart. This way, they would stay there forever, and you would remain together forever.

CLIENT: Oh, my God . . . how did you know? This is what we did! It was his idea. I thought it was silly at the time, but he insisted. But that was four days before Peter died, and I have never told anyone about it to this day!

LISA: He's showing me that you will always be in his heart, now and forever.

CLIENT: [shaking and crying through her tears] I just finished having those words written on a headstone for his grave: *He will be in my heart, now and forever.*

This story illustrates the way in which we mediums can present a message when it's first received. There are times we don't always get a message right or say it in a way that our clients can relate to. But if we tell someone what we heard and saw and then simply leave it to the person to make sense of it, the message will often get through very powerfully. Problems occur when mediums receive symbols and then force their own emotions into the mix (something we should never do), giving a message that is not relatable and that only confuses the person.

I often get the symbol of a red rose, which many people relate to as a symbol of love. I'll say, "I'm getting a red rose," and leave it to the individuals to respond. They may say, "Oh, my grandmother's name was Rose." Or, "He gave me red roses all the time on our anniversary." However, to me personally, a red rose symbolizes a birthday. If I offer someone my own interpretation of this symbol, he or she might question the information—so I have to take it one step further to help the person relate to it better.

This is what happened in my reading with my client Cathy, who came to see me after her son passed. You'll be able to see how offering my own understanding can sometimes be helpful, and also how the symbol for a birthday can relate to the experience of a soul in the Afterlife:

LISA: Your son is showing me that there is a birthday around this period of time.

CATHY: [looking puzzled] No, his birthday is in six months.

LISA: Hmm, okay. Well, he's showing me a red rose. To me, that symbolizes a birthday. It could be an anniversary, but it feels like an event that has to do with him, not anyone else.

CATHY: Well, it is the anniversary of his death tomorrow.

LISA: That's it! *You* see his time of passing as an anniversary of his death, but to him it's a birthday. This can only mean he's trying to tell you that he has been reborn into the spirit world.

The symbol of a red rose was the way Cathy's son chose to communicate how he saw the anniversary of his passing—that is, as a rebirth. He wanted to convey that he had returned back to his true home to begin a new "life." He was reborn in the Afterlife! This is why Josiah says that life is enabled by death. He and the other spirits view death as the point at which human life and lessons are just beginning.

You'll understand all of this more as we explore the healing process of the Afterlife in future chapters. But for now, here is a message from Josiah about the rebirth awaiting us all when we die:

> *The White Light of love and purity leads to the Afterlife, heaven, or whatever you would like to call it. It is a land of peace, calm, and commitment. Yes, commitment—for when you pass and have crossed to the Light, you are committing yourself to learning, growing, and developing to become a better soul.*

I find it very interesting that Josiah says there is a commitment in the Afterlife to learning and growing, since many of us tend to shy away from consciously learning and growing on the Earth plane. Yet although we might prefer to take the slow lane for a more comfortable ride, we never stop getting opportunities to learn and grow in life.

Life *and* the Afterlife—both are all about growth and learning. *Life enabled by death* can be a hard concept to grasp because we think that the Afterlife is a place where we finally get to relax, rest, and have fun. While that is the case, there is so much more to it —which you'll discover as we move along in the book.

The Welcome Home

Previously, I mentioned that when you first arrive in the After-life, you spend time in the Meeting Room, a kind of threshold in which you're placed before moving on. It is here that you meet up with all of your soul connections, and there is a lot of joy, just as if you were attending a reunion with family members and friends you haven't seen in a long time.

Ben describes how the spirits who have helped and guided you on the Earth plane take on a new role after they welcome you home:

Their job from now on is to show you that this journey of life after death is not one that should be feared; rather, it should be embraced. These spirits will be accompanied by your master guide, whom you will know very well, regardless of if you were acquainted with him or her in your earthly life. Together, this team will lead you to the place you are destined to go.

Many of the spirits on your team have been assigned tasks to help you through your transition. Once you have completed that transition, then you will also be assigned a task when it is time for you to welcome a loved one back home. Such tasks are simple: to love, support, and guide a soul through the stages of rebirth in the Afterlife.

Some of these spirits will assist your master guide in helping you cope with the people and circumstances left on the Earth plane after your passing. Since certain souls cope better with this than others, your master guide works with them to see that they have the right jobs to provide the most help.

What Ben is describing here is the mixture of emotions you'll experience when you pass. Your senses will be heightened, of course, so everything will be more intense than you may be used to. You will probably still have strong feelings about those you left behind on the Earth plane; that's because you still have your earthly ties and the associated emotions at this point. You will have to closely observe these earthly ties and emotions and deal with them over a period of time. But for now, you need only to focus on getting your bearings, allowing yourself to be guided into your new home gently.

You may be wondering, *How can I embrace my loved ones in the Afterlife when I have no body?* That is a good question, and I'll try to answer it in a satisfactory way. In life, we all have an aura around our body, which extends out farther than most of us are aware. As we become close in proximity to each other, our auras naturally start to merge. Those of us who are sensitive to energy will pick up others' feelings and desires. This happens all the time in earthly life, but isn't always recognized for what it is.

Since there are no bodies in the Afterlife, an even greater transfer of energy occurs when two souls embrace. Try to imagine that you're the source of all the energy you feel, with no dense body to filter those feelings (which is in fact how it is in the Afterlife); your senses will be very sharp. As pure energy, you can merge with the other energy sources around you, becoming one as you embrace. This is a very powerful experience, and in this way, you embrace and greet each and every one of the souls with whom you are reconnecting.

Also, you communicate with others in thoughts and only have to think for them to "hear" you. This answers another question that many people ask me: "Do I have to talk out loud in order for my loved ones to hear me, or can I think the thoughts to them?" You can absolutely think your thoughts, and your loved ones will instantly pick up on them. Again, there is no dense physical body to interfere with the transmission of energy.

Being in the Meeting Room is an extraordinary and beautiful experience. You feel at peace, enjoying a bliss that you could only imagine on Earth. When I experienced being in this place during my near-death experience, it was enlightening, captivating, serene, calm, tranquil . . . and just about every other glorious sensation that you can imagine. You will feel all of this and even more when you visit this place for yourself.

You'll stay in the Meeting Room for a period of time—but as I've already mentioned, time in the Afterlife is a vastly different concept than we're used to. What will feel like hours in the Afterlife is only a minute on Earth, which I know is not easy to understand. For ease of comprehension, I will try to explain the process in both timescales as we go along.

The journey of your rebirth in the Afterlife is now about to begin. But first, in preparation for the full healing process your soul will experience, you're given the opportunity to return to the Earth plane and visit with those you left behind.

Please note that the purpose of your visit back is not to re-connect in ways that strengthen your earthly bonds. Rather, you'll be taken back by your guides so that you can begin the important and sometimes difficult task of *detaching from* your earthly ties. Only then will your full rebirth in the Afterlife begin.

CHAPTER 9

DETACHING FROM EARTHLY TIES

Once we've been gently accepted into our new home, greeted and embraced by all those who have guided and loved us (and will now guide us forward), we begin the process of separating from the people and situations we were closely tied to over the course of our life on Earth. All we need to do is think of whom we wish to see, and our team of souls will help us visit each one we need to. This is important for us to do, since it's part of our larger severing of earthly ties, which must happen before our formal process of healing can begin in the Afterlife.

Detaching from earthly ties is an essential process for every soul to go through—we *all* have to do it. When we pass, we'll still be thinking in our incarnated form, identifying ourselves as a male or female, having a name that we were called in life, and holding on to emotions toward people we knew. All of these and more are our attachments that keep us tied to our earthly existence, acting like an anchor that holds us back from our progress in the Afterlife, our journey of rebirth.

Ariel gives details of the first step in the detachment process covered in this chapter:

It's natural for every soul who crosses over to start off his or her rebirth in the Afterlife with a trip back to the Earth plane. It is a trip that all souls need to make, sometimes many times, to clarify what has happened and to be assured that loved ones left behind are all right. This helps the souls detach from their earthly bonds, which we help them do as their guides in the process. We provide whatever they need for a visit with those they have left behind, but are careful not to let them get stuck.

The First Trip Back

You will probably want to return to the Earth plane almost as soon as you pass, since you'll be fully aware of what is going on there and still feel very close to the people you've just left. You'll be distracted by the grief that is surrounding your loved ones, as well as by all the activities surrounding your passing, but you'll also be anticipating the next stage of the Afterlife. Everything is happening at a very fast pace compared to what you're used to, and this can be disorienting.

I've heard this early experience of the Afterlife described lots of times by many spirits who have come through to communicate. Here's how Ben puts it:

> *We take you on a journey, a journey home. First we show you around the Afterlife, but you are not allowed to stop anywhere or become involved. You see it all from a distance, as if you were flying around the perimeter, looking down from a bird's-eye view. You see the love that is here and the way that we all support and guide each other. You watch the intricate network and the freedom we have. This is when you realize you want to stay here.*
>
> *As part of that journey, we also take you to the Earth plane to visit your family members and friends who are now grieving. Other members of your support team go with you, providing the energy you need to give signs to your loved ones that you are still with them. You also give them the comforting message that you have been received in the Afterlife and are safe.*
>
> *They miss you, but you do not experience missing them. You love them and want them to be well, but you will never miss them like they miss you. That is because you can return to their world when you need to, or if they call upon you for help.*

For your growth process, it is imperative that you witness what they are going through and understand what they are feeling. Only by being completely present with them in an honest and open way can you complete your relationships on the Earth plane and then release them so that you can move on. This is how you begin to detach from your worldly ties, and it is just the start of the journey over to the other side.

Your first trip back to the Earth plane is the easiest one you will make, as you have lots of energy at this time. The White Light you went through when crossing over acts as an energy source, propelling you to communicate in ways that let your loved ones know you're still around. You'll come back and watch the final plans for your funeral or memorial, witnessing every emotion. It can be frustrating, as you're in another dimension and will want to jump up and down in front of people, shouting, *Hey, can't you see me?! I'm fine!*

You might think that you wouldn't want to return to the scene of your passing, but all souls are asked to watch and be part of that process for emotional healing. And because you're still tied to the Earth plane, chances are you're going to want to make the visit—particularly if you didn't get to say good-bye because your passing happened quickly or tragically.

You'll be able to see your physical body, which of course is now removed from your spirit. You'll also see things such as people running into the room who didn't make it in time to be with you for your final breath. These individuals are now processing feelings of guilt; and you'll be able to hear their conversations, feel their emotions, and hear their thoughts as they gather around your body.

Joining your loved ones, you'll be able to stand close to them and try to alleviate the pain they're feeling as a result of your passing. Their grief can be overwhelming, but it's something you'll become accustomed to. You may even want to be part of what they're experiencing because it helps you accept what has happened.

It's not unusual for those left behind to want you to show yourself to them in your earthly form. Yet it can be exhausting to make an appearance "in the flesh," as it takes an incredible amount of energy to do so. Also, there is no good time for you to do it—because even though they may see you, it will be such a shock that they might turn away. By the time they did a double take, you'd be gone, disappearing right in front of their eyes. This could evoke emotions of regret that are intensified by grief . . . so for these reasons, such appearances are very rare.

Ariel gives more detail about this:

> We who have passed have to use an enormous amount of energy to show ourselves physically. It is much easier to influence those on Earth to listen to certain songs, signaling them to turn on the radio when they normally would not. Then we can put a thought in through their guide to get them to listen at a certain time to a recording or show. But for us to stand "revealed" before them is what people want most of all, and it is not as easy as you would think. Our energy level is so much higher than theirs because the Afterlife exists at a higher frequency. In our dimension, we have to work hard at lowering our vibrations to match theirs. It takes a while to master this, and some do not master it at all, because they do not wish to be part of the earthly life anymore.

Your team of helpers will show you the way to communicate during this first visit back to the Earth plane, teaching you several ways to get your messages through. You can influence your loved ones to take notice of a piece of music, to look down and see a penny or a dime in the street with a special date on it, or to listen to words spoken by a stranger that refer to something personal. All of this is done through a transfer of energy and thought processes, impacting the physical world from the spirit realm.

The easiest way of communicating with those on the Earth plane is while they sleep. You'll be able to tap into their dreams easily and spend time with their souls, and they'll wake up feeling as if you've been with them. The reality is, you have. Your souls will be connected: as they leave their body through the natural sleep process and astral-travel, you'll be able to meet with them and talk, and even have fun together.

All communication is an important part of the healing you're doing at this stage in the Afterlife, and it's very natural to do. Think about when you leave for a trip and you're going to be away from those you care about. When you arrive at your destination, you want to check in with them—either through a phone call, text message, or e-mail—just to say, "Hey, I arrived. The weather is great, and the room is fabulous. I'll see you in two weeks. Have fun!" We all do this—it's part of human nature for us to be concerned about each other, and to want to put each other's minds at ease.

∽

It is normal for you as a soul to stay very close to the Earth plane for a while in order to do whatever it takes to cut your worldly ties. It's important to be around for the final celebrations of your life, witness your own funeral, and see the changes to the family dynamics or people sorting out your estate and your belongings. This is all part of your coming to terms with the fact that you have crossed over. You'll see the arguments and the sadness that your passing has created. You'll also see the laughter of your loved ones as they look through old photographs and remember the funny things you did.

All of this is part of your growth process, your rebirth. It's typical to stay around the Earth plane in the human sense of time for up to 90 days, which is like half a day in the Afterlife. The amount of time differs depending on the soul, since every soul has different needs.

While you're visiting, it can be very tempting to stay longer—but keep in mind that it's extremely difficult for you to move on through the Afterlife if you're still clinging to guilt and feel your loved ones constantly calling for you, making you want to stay. Eventually, you're going to have to let go of such earthly emotions. You'll come to understand that you will have other opportunities to resolve your heaviest issues when you go through the next stage of the healing process in the Afterlife.

Even though you may leave and return to the Afterlife after your first trip back, it doesn't mean that you won't be visiting again. You can come back to the Earth plane and be with your loved ones at any time. As Ariel states:

> In the first stages of rebirth, souls will go back often because they are still thinking in the earthly form. So it is important for them to have that connection. The loved ones who were left behind are still wanting the souls—and, in many cases, _needing_ them—to be there for them. We try to help this process, but what new souls forget is that they cannot always do things in the way they would like to. As their guides, we have to tell them that they are wasting energy by staying so connected to the earthly life and not using their energy for their own healing. But we recognize that visiting is an important part of acceptance on this side of life. Souls can choose to go back as often as they would like to, to help out and influence their loved ones' grieving process.

Your spirit guides will always be available to help you take trips back to be around those people you associated with in life, so you can learn what they thought of you and how you impacted their lives. All of this is preparing you for the next step on your healing journey in the Afterlife. But it is important to continually follow the lead of your helpers at this stage, letting them guide you to stay or leave, as they ultimately know what's best for you. You do have free will as always, and you can stay longer if you need to, but don't waste energy that is better spent on your own healing.

Ariel has this to say:

> Some souls go back more times than others. Some do not go back at all, as they have made their peace and are ready to accept their fate and move on. But visiting too often or staying too long can be a disadvantage, since it holds a soul back from its further learning in the Afterlife. In the earthly time frame, one step forward to you is two steps back in the soul's development.

On your first trip back to the Earth plane, you're guided completely by your team of helpers who have your best interests at heart. They want to help you slowly release all the emotions and ties you have to your life before . . . but your departed loved ones may find it hard to accept that you must do so. Nevertheless, completing your relationships and finally freeing yourself from your worldly ties is a necessary step for you to move on in your Afterlife journey.

Letting Go and Moving On

As a recently passed soul, it's vital that you sever all ties that keep you living in your physicality with an ego, focused on the material things around you—no matter how big *or* small. You have to fully live in the soul and let go of the things that mattered to you when you were incarnate, such as cars, houses, TV shows, and other things that you liked and wanted in your life as a human. (That's why when a spirit comes through to a medium, it won't talk about money, but rather laugh and point out, *You've been spending money,* because it's been watching.)

Releasing is part of all souls' growth process in the Afterlife. But be assured that as a soul, you won't lose the emotions you have toward people on the Earth plane. You won't lose memories of special moments either—those memories are important for your growth as well, since you'll pull on them to get your lessons in your next life.

However, other things that were once important to you will no longer mean anything. For instance, material objects or belongings have no value now. Labels of any sort also drop away, and this includes nicknames or even first names. In the Afterlife, you revert back to your original soul name, which is your true name. As I mentioned in an earlier chapter, for years my son, Charlie, insisted that I call him "Sam," since this was the name he'd had in "heaven."

Ariel explains more about what souls do hang on to:

Earthly folk would like you to remember certain things in life when you come back to communicate with them, such as their favorite piece of music and their favorite color. But that is not what is significant.

As a soul, you do not lose your personality; it remains with you. What you remember are significant things, such as the instances of learning in your life and the memories of family members. You will especially treasure and keep with you the moments that changed your life. The rest are not relevant. It sounds harsh, but this is how it is. You only keep hold of what is truly important.

I must point out here that while souls generally remain in touch with those on the Earth plane, some don't want to return and show their loved ones any signs of their presence. As a person left behind, you may feel very unhappy and upset about not getting any visits. It's hard to accept that someone you love is just "gone." But what you must understand is that when dealing with a soul, you're dealing with a personality. If someone was stubborn in life, that individual will still be stubborn in the Afterlife, especially when he or she has just crossed over, because of the strong association with earthly ties.

There are many reasons why souls may not want to visit or make their presence known to grieving family and friends: some are struggling with their own passing, despite the preparations that they went through; others don't want to come back because it's too painful for them to see the grief of those they left behind; and still others have said their last good-byes and are eager to move up through the realms of the Afterlife. You need to think about what your departed loved one was like in life, which will help explain his or her presence (or lack thereof) in the time shortly after passing.

Natasha's Story

I've had many personal experiences of a soul coming back shortly after passing on, and even though I should be used to such events, they still surprise me. The following story shows how a soul can return to the Earth plane in what seemed like a very short time after passing. It taught me that the impact of such a visit can be huge, as the visiting soul has the ability to influence a loved one for the better and help him or her move on in life. I think it is a beautiful account, and the perfect way to end this chapter.

My dear friend Frankie Leigh had a niece by marriage named Natasha Shneider, who was a famous singer and songwriter in Russia and the U.S. Natasha had been battling cancer for a while, so on Frankie's recommendation, she started to come to me for healing—then, through the final stages of her illness, I visited her in her home. Even though she wasn't conscious at the time, I was able to communicate with her as I did with my Nan Frances when she was preparing to pass, solely through my thoughts. Interestingly enough, Natasha had showed me that she wanted to help her husband, Alain Johannes, follow his passion in the music industry, and I passed that information on to him.

Natasha had fought her illness long and hard, but at one point I had to tell Frankie that her niece wasn't going to pull through this. The healing I was doing wasn't helping her body, but it was helping her soul prepare to make the transition over to the other side. Alain, Frankie, and the rest of the family had to come to terms with the fact that they would be losing their dear loved one soon.

I was leaving for England and went to see Natasha on my way to the airport. I knew it would be the last time I saw her, and I felt guilty that I wouldn't be able to help her soul make that final transition. Once I arrived in England, I visited my local Spiritualist church, Studley Spiritual Group, and sat in the audience while a medium onstage delivered messages to people. I felt a presence and suddenly had the urge to check my phone. There was the text that I'd been dreading.

Natasha sang in a band called Eleven, and she had passed away at 11:11, peacefully in her sleep. I had to leave the room for a short period to compose myself, and when I returned, the medium honed in on me and started to deliver a brief message from Natasha. On the way home, I stopped off at the store. Coming back to my car, I suddenly saw Natasha sitting in the passenger seat, smiling her beautiful smile and looking radiant. I closed my eyes and received a message from her for Alain, her devoted husband, saying that even though she'd passed, she would always be there for him and help him with his dreams.

This is not an unusual event for me, to have a spirit visit shortly after passing. To that end, Natasha popped in because she knew I'd deliver her message directly to Alain. It was her way of saying, *Look, I'm here, and I'm fine!* Here is the exact message that I texted through to Alain, which Natasha had given me: *Peaceful, no pain, and it felt good to go. Love you all and thank you. It was easier than I thought. Be strong, baby.*

Alain now plays with a group called Them Crooked Vultures, traveling throughout the world as a successful musician. Jointly, Natasha and Alain wrote the song "Time for Miracles," which was recently recorded by American Idol contestant and rising pop star Adam Lambert. Every time something amazing happens in Alain's career, the family all says in unison, "That's Natasha!"

I hope that these last few chapters have given you an idea of what to expect as you cross over from the Earth plane. Now, Part III takes you through the stages of your life on the other side, a time when you will focus on embracing all that has happened in your life on Earth, accepting it and being complete with people and events. Through this process, and with the support of your spirit team, you will experience your rebirth in the Afterlife.

PART III

THE HEALING JOURNEY

CHAPTER 10

INITIATION: THE WAITING ROOM

Once you return from your first visit back to the Earth plane, you begin your initiation into the healing journey of the Afterlife. You've been prepared for this by crossing over through the veil and into the White Light, meeting your soul connections, and detaching from your earthly ties. Each of these events has been carefully planned and structured to help you move along in your evolution as a soul.

Ariel explains how crucial the healing journey is:

Healing is an important process all souls must go through during their stay in the Afterlife—because of the hurt, heartache, suffering, or illness endured in earthly life—and it is not easy. But it is a necessary part of rebirth and must be undertaken before a soul is allowed to transcend into the higher realms for deeper learning in a more spiritual dimension.

Many souls cross over to this side believing that they have led a spiritual life and therefore have spiritual understanding, but this is not usually so. Once initiated into the healing process, their eyes are metaphorically opened, and they see the light. Our job is to allow for an understanding of what souls are here to accomplish. This is something we cannot do for them, for it is part of their healing process.

Some souls arrive in the Afterlife needing to heal physically from the pain and suffering they endured in the body—and their energetic body, or aura, is often in need of repair as well. If they arrive here in a weakened condition, that can explain why

*their first visit back to the Earth plane is kept short. These souls
must gain strength in order to cope with the healing process and
be ready to learn and understand their life lessons.*

On your own journey, every step is vital for your evolution. Of
course, your team of helpers will be guiding you, and it's important
that you follow their advice. Even though you've gone through this
process before when you crossed over in your previous incarnations, you can easily forget what it's like. Missing any of the steps
can impact your life when you return back to the Earth plane,
affecting the way you lead and embrace your next life.

Your soul is constantly changing, growing, and learning, so
you have to follow the process that is planned for you. It's not
always the easiest thing to do—the healing stage is something that
many souls don't particularly like to do. But as you read about it
now, *before* it's your time, your views may change about how you
live your life and deal with people. That in itself would be a part of
your healing process . . . and it is true that healing is fundamental
in this life as well as in the Afterlife.

Healing on Both Planes

The healing process on the Earth plane is very similar to what
you must do in the Afterlife. In life, you need to repair yourself after
damaging or disappointing relationships, financial catastrophes,
addictions—all the negative situations that being human throws
at you. You naturally take time to grieve, and then at some point
you're ready to move on.

There is no right or wrong way to deal with a negative situation,
but it's best not to ignore it or allow it to fester inside you. Better to
actively remove those blocks that stop you in life so that you may
continue to grow. How many times have you made a decision to
walk away from a bad relationship, for instance, and then suddenly
your life changed and something more positive occurred? As the
saying goes, when one door closes, another opens.

You can prepare for your healing journey in the Afterlife by spiritually enriching your life on the Earth plane as much as possible. Your ego is a factor in this because it can get in the way of your understanding and living a fundamental spiritual truth—which is that your life is exactly as it was destined. It's difficult for the ego to accept that *all is as it should be.*

When your ego influences your every decision and choice, your spiritual growth becomes impeded. You can circumvent your ego by embracing all that life gives you and valuing it all—even the hard stuff—since it's given to you for a reason and a purpose. Know that you yourself planned this life exactly the way it has turned out, setting it all up before you came to this planet as part of the plan for your evolving soul. Acknowledging this reality will make life on Earth and in the Afterlife go more smoothly and be so much more enjoyable.

As earthly humans, we're always looking for ways to make our life better and searching for what we think is lacking. The grass may look greener on someone else's lawn, but often it is not. The truth is that whatever you have at this particular moment—your possessions, your relationships, and your circumstances, no matter how difficult—is exactly what you were meant to have. For me, at this point in time, I can say that I have everything I need. As I sit here writing, I have music to listen to, my laptop to work on, my sight, my ability to type, my knowledge of the Afterlife, my team of helpers, and the love in my heart that supports me every moment in writing this book. I find nothing lacking!

When *you* are able to embrace the reality that in any given moment you have everything you need, you'll find a way to be happy with what you have. It's not about having the luxuries in life, such as the biggest diamond, the latest season's fashions, or the swankiest house. Instead, it's about having love in your heart, and that comes from accepting that you have the perfect lot in life for you—regardless of what it is. This is what you'll eventually have to accept as you undergo your healing journey in the Afterlife. Life is about love, not material things.

Some men and women feel that their lives are too difficult, that they're the victims of life. And yes, some people do have more challenges to deal with than others do. But as you read on in this book, you'll discover that you're actually only given that which you choose. You chose your life for a reason, and it's important for you to realize this. You never need to look at others and be jealous of their material possessions; in reality, you may in fact be a lot happier, and your life may be much more full of love.

With this understanding, your transition through the healing stages of the other side and the rest of the journey will be much easier. As in earthly life, so it is in the Afterlife, requiring that you surrender to what you have and accept that you're always in the right place at the right time. You have all the information that you need to know right now—nothing is hidden or withheld—and you'll always be given exactly what you need at the time you need it.

∽

Here, Ben talks about looking within ourselves for answers during life, and how this inner search is connected to our healing progress on the other side:

> *We are all given help along the way, but some choose not to accept that help and experience a difficult life as a result. Of course, you have free will and can choose what you like, but you will come to realize that your life is hard because you have not searched within for the help and the answers that are there.*
>
> *You may say that you have done this, but have you? You might have read a book and tried to still your mind and stop the endless chatter of your thoughts and feelings. But have you chosen to see with open eyes, to examine your life and question every aspect using the guidance we give you?*
>
> *Looking within means that you have the courage to see into your motives, your desires, your deepest fears—the full range of it—with nothing hidden, nothing denied. But not everyone wants to look that deep. It is one of the hardest things to do as well as the least comfortable. This why so many people struggle*

and say that life is tough, life is hard. They have not gone deep within and truly found themselves. Their lives may be very externally focused, arranged to please others instead of themselves, so they never have to look within. Even if they did attempt this, they would not like the answers they found, because those answers might force them to change and step outside of their comfort zone.

The fact is, you are going to have to look within and responsibly face all that you have ignored at some point. If you are putting that process off until D-day comes, then you are putting off the inevitable, and it will only be harder on you to do then.

It is never easy, but you must do this inner work in life to move forward—or do it in the Afterlife, where it will be required of you on your healing journey. When you examine your life then, all your senses will be heightened and your emotions alive, so you will truly feel whatever you were not present for in life. So why not feel it now on the Earth plane? Why shy away from this?

Sometimes life is hard, but the toughest situations are always the ones that actually help us, if we're willing to honestly examine our lives. This is the path to ultimate happiness, both here and in the Afterlife. So many times I've personally found myself in circumstances that I thought would make me happy but didn't. Now I see that I had to go through those difficult experiences because they made me realize what I truly needed and wanted—and then, with my new awareness, I got it! *Doors close and doors open* is a simple truth we must understand to be happy.

What has all this got to do with the survival of the soul? Put simply, it's only human to go through difficult and painful situations, because that's how we learn and grow. It's exactly the same on the other side. In other words, everything you go through in your life will help you in the Afterlife.

Furthermore, the healing you go through in the Afterlife will release all the negativity you experienced on the Earth plane. But in order for this to happen, you will have to access your life and analyze it closely—a process that starts with a look at your original Life Contract as described later in this chapter. Once you've advanced on your healing journey, you become free to transcend through the higher realms of the other side with a pure soul, enriched from love and no longer tainted by the negativity that hurt you in life.

Overview of the Journey

Now I'd like to give you an overview of the full healing journey, using a fun analogy I often employ.

Imagine a department store such as a Macy's or a Sears. Like the Afterlife, this type of store has many different areas for the flow of incoming goods to move through, from arrival to eventual placement. So it is in the Afterlife, as souls progress along a continuum of healing and growth.

Some of you reading this may take offense at this example, finding it to be disrespectful. But I've been using it for many years to assist those on the Earth plane in understanding the process of crossing over and the healing journey. On many occasions while giving a reading, I've even heard my guides say, *Tell them the department-store analogy* . . . so I do. It helps people keep the whole of the Afterlife in mind and is also an easy way of understanding the lay of the land. So if you can, please put aside any offense for the sake of clarity and understanding.

One other important point before I proceed with the analogy: In a department store, the flow of goods from manufacturer to floor display follows a linear progression, from A to B to C, while the actual experience of the soul in the Afterlife is anything but linear. Instead, the soul's real progress is *cyclical*, meaning that its movements include many turnarounds. A soul may move from A to B, then back to A before going on to C. Such cyclical progression is the path all healing takes, whether on the Earth plane or in the Afterlife. Keep this greater truth in mind as you read this section—and also in future chapters where the healing path is described—as it relies on a linear progression to get my point across.

So, using the analogy, every department store has an area where newly arrived goods are received, usually a loading bay of some sort. Similarly, in the Meeting Room of the Afterlife, newly arrived souls are received by their team of helpers after crossing through the White Light, as you've read about previously.

Back at the store, goods are entered and checked in from the loading bay, a process known as "stock control." Then an inventory is done so the store knows what's been received in a shipment. For souls in the Afterlife, the Waiting Room is their entry or initiation into the healing journey. Here, souls undergo an inventory of what they have and have not accomplished in life, checked against agreements made before birth, or their Life Contract.

Once goods in the store are checked in and inventory is taken, they're moved into a warehouse area to be held for sorting before going out to the sales floor. As a soul in the Afterlife, you'll spend time in a holding area called the "Viewing Room," where you'll sort out every aspect of the life you just left. Here, you'll do your Life Review and have a chance to right the wrongs you've committed on the Earth plane.

In the department store, goods that are sorted are ready to be moved onto the floor for placement in the appropriate departments. In the Afterlife, souls who have completed their Life Review are ready to move on to different healing rooms for more advanced work, so they can continue to learn and grow.

The healing journey almost complete, souls arrive at the Guardianship Room, which is similar to where managers work and have their offices in a department store. In the Afterlife, this is the level of the Elders and other highly evolved entities, whose job it is to help souls assess their progress and make plans for a future course in the Afterlife. For those returning to the Earth plane, there is the Screening Room, which is analogous to a place in the store where returned goods are gathered for eventual replacement. Souls in the Screening Room are prepared for reincarnation and allowed to view and choose possible parents and situations for their next earthly sojourn.

Beyond the Guardianship Room and the Screening Room is the huge expanse of the Afterlife, including the domains of angels and God, a place I refer to as the Source. For this, there is no earthly analogy, so I won't attempt to make one!

The Initiation Begins

The beginning of your formal healing journey takes place in the Waiting Room. You remain here until it is your turn to be called, and to be shown your original Life Contract. These are the agreements you made with Spirit before you entered your previous earthly life.

Here, you'll also be checked in and assigned to go with your group of like souls to various healing paths and rooms. Going back to my department-store analogy, after being checked in, goods are grouped together and sent on to various sections in the store. For example, women's hats are routed in one direction, while men's shoes go in another. So it is with souls: you are routed with your group to the appropriate place. There is no apprehension involved in this process, as all the love you felt when you crossed over is still with you, a condition that never changes.

As you await your turn to be checked in, there are opportunities for you to become accustomed to the experience of the Afterlife. I've mentioned how time moves faster and activity is sped up on the other side, to the point that that if you witnessed the Afterlife with human eyes, you'd only see a blur of forms whizzing by at very high speeds.

You may have noted this phenomenon while still in your body, catching tiny sparks out of the corner of your eye. This is a sign that spirits are trying to communicate with you by signaling you in your peripheral vision. Unlike a soul, a body must first react to what the eyes are seeing, then register it in the brain to send a message to the muscles. When muscles react, humans act or express an emotion. The mechanics of our human form slow down what is a fast process for souls who are freed from corporality.

There are other phenomena to get used to in the Afterlife, such as the lack of night or day. Souls do not need to sleep, but if they want to rest, they can. Even though they're attached to our world, they're in a totally different dimension and therefore don't have a need for night and day. Souls have no gender either, so there are no male or female souls—but they still retain certain aspects of their earthly personalities.

A wonderful thing about the Afterlife is that there is no hostility or danger; it's peaceful and calm. You'll find the atmosphere to be welcoming at all times, assuring you that there is nothing to fear. However, you have your own unique state of mind that comes with you. So whatever you decide that state of mind is, you will create your experience from it, just as you did on the Earth plane. As a result, you can project a negative state of mind and then receive that negativity back. Likewise, if you put out positive energy, you'll get positivity back. *Like attracts like* is a rule in the Afterlife just as it is on Earth.

Ben shares the following comments to further explain what happens during your stay in the Waiting Room:

> *Your guides will take you to be checked in for the healing journey in the Afterlife. While this process may take a while, you must remember that time as you know it on the Earth plane is not the same here. There is no essence of time; it is never ending.*
>
> *You are given a checklist of items taken from the original contract you made before you returned back to Earth for your most recent incarnation. On this checklist are all the things you agreed to achieve in life, the lessons you agreed to learn, the individuals you agreed to help and who would help you. It also includes the people who were to impact your life (and how they would do it), the good deeds and the wrongdoings that you would do, the health issues you would face and the recovery that you would have, your financial losses and gains, the loves to come in and out of your life . . . everything that you were supposed to achieve will be on that checklist as taken from your*

Life Contract. Added are the extra things you accomplished throughout your time of being on the Earth plane that were not in your original contract.

All of this is written on your checklist, and you must deal with it all in the next phase of your healing, the Life Review, to ensure that you move on in your healing journey.

Fulfilling Your Contract and Destiny

In the Waiting Room you are greeted by an Elder, a guiding spirit who holds your Life Contract. When I was introduced to Josiah, he told me that the term *Elder* was only a label and that he didn't consider himself to be of a higher status than any other soul. Josiah made it clear that he still has growth and learning to accomplish, as all do in the Afterlife—but he is a highly evolved soul chosen to take on the role of checking in new souls as they're initiated into the Afterlife, as well as other duties I will relate in a future chapter.

As Ben channeled in the previous section, your Life Contract contains the lessons that you committed yourself to learn during your time on the Earth plane. We all have such a contract, an agreement we drew up with the help of our Elder and our spirit guides to record and confirm the lessons we will be learning.

Because your contract is set for life, your incarnation is predestined before you're even born. However, you still have free will to make choices and decisions that aren't in your contract. To understand what seems to be a contradiction—predestination and free will—follow me through an imaginary scenario.

Imagine that you're out running errands, and you drop off a prescription at the pharmacy. In the time it takes for the prescription to be filled, you decide to do some shopping. As you're coming out of a store, about to head back to the pharmacy, you run into an old friend whom you haven't seen for a while. The two of you decide to get some coffee and catch up on each other's lives. Ultimately, the predestined plan is to pick up your prescription—but by virtue of your free will, you altered that plan when you chose to go have coffee with your old friend.

Some may question if the meeting with your friend was actually free will or if it was meant to happen—in other words, predestination. But whether your friend was part of the plan or not doesn't matter, since you always have a choice to do something different. Think of it this way: collecting your prescription is the part that's predestined, but *when* and *how* you decide to collect it is up to you. This is similar to the contract you make in the Afterlife, which requires many things to be accomplished—but there will always be tests along the way, and you'll forever be making choices thanks to your free will.

∽

Your Life Contract is sacred, something that must be honored. At your check-in with an Elder, you'll look at the list of those agreements from your contract that you didn't accomplish and still need to achieve. Included in those agreements, you'll also see people who are important, those who are your teachers on the Earth plane and in the Afterlife. These will most often be individuals who have been part of your soul family over many lifetimes, especially those who are sent to make an impact in your life. For example, you may have a contract that involves an individual with whom you have a romantic relationship. You might not last as a couple, but you still have to fulfill the terms of your contract with that person, completing any lessons you've agreed to learn with him or her.

Let me explain this further with a very personal example. In one of my past lives, I became pregnant by a man who today is Simon, my son's father. In that life, he didn't want me to have the child, and neither did my mother (who was not my mother in this life). Yielding to their pressure, I agreed to a backstreet abortion against my will, and since it was in the days when there was no anesthetic for such operations, it was very painful. Due to complications from the procedure, which caused an infection in my pelvic area that spread throughout my body, it eventually took my life.

Now all of this is interesting, because in this life I've had serious medical problems in my pelvic area. Even though I'd been told for many years I would not be able to have children because of my pelvic problems and other medical conditions, the miracle happened when Simon and I got together: I became pregnant.

Also interesting is that my mother in this life wanted me to think twice before I made up my mind to have the baby, as I'd just gotten out of one relationship, and she was naturally worried about me starting another. But I figured it would be my one and only chance to have a child, so I decided to keep the pregnancy and have Charlie. (I was right that it was my only chance; I had a hysterectomy not long after he was born.)

Even though Simon and I are no longer together, we do have a good relationship, having overcome so many difficulties that we've both encountered. As souls who have shared many lifetimes, our contract required that we meet again in this life and have a child together. I believe that Simon and I were destined to take on parenthood, both in this life and the last one, to help us face up to our responsibilities. I also believe that Charlie chose us as parents because we could provide him with the lessons he needed to impact many others with his own spiritual gifts. And I can honestly, hand-on-heart tell you that this boy has saved my life on more than one occasion.

I was supposed to be a parent and grow from the experience, coming to understand people better and appreciate how to love and be responsible. All of this was arranged in my contract, and I chose my life—as you have chosen yours—before I came to the Earth plane, based on what I needed to accomplish in this incarnation and what I had to complete from past ones.

Your own Life Contract is an agreement you cannot get out of —it binds you over many lifetimes. You are led through all of these lifetimes by your guides, who, unbeknownst to you, place you in situations you may or may not want to be in but are necessary to bring about the next monumental events to fulfill your contract. You'll be placed "coincidentally" with people who will change your life, but none of these are truly coincidences. You're being led and guided according to a plan that will help you fulfill your contract to the best of your ability. If you surrender to the universe and don't force issues in life, you'll fulfill your contract in such a way that is how it was meant to be.

Meeting those with whom you've made a contract for some specific accomplishment isn't always obvious or easy. For example, I recently met someone who I know is part of my Life Contract, as I am part of theirs, yet we still haven't discovered fully what our work together is. We both know that by coming together, we will help many people, yet we had to laugh because we met at a time of change for me, which created a great deal of turmoil for us both, and the timing seemed too far off for us to do anything meaningful together. As much as we would have liked our relationship to be smoother, the actuality was that we were being tested to see if we could get through the obstacles and work together this time, completing both our contracts by lessons learned from our two pathways crossing.

In a short amount of time, it's possible to learn so many lessons to influence the rest of your life. Keeping your mind open to spirituality or having faith will especially help you in fulfilling your contract. Note that faith is not about a religion so much as believing in who you are and that you can achieve what you so desire, as long as it's for your own higher purpose and you don't walk over others to achieve it.

Looking within for your answers is key to the guidance that is available throughout your whole life. Meditation is also a key practice for life, because if you can live in the present and slow down your mind to focus on the less material matters, you'll be given all the tools for growth and achieve what you set out to do.

In closing, Ben reminds us of the importance of looking within to understand life:

> *Meditation is the key that gives you access to all the knowledge and understanding of life, certainly to the life you lead now and also to the many others you have led before.*

There is a whole universe waiting for you to explore, but you will never know the meaning of it all, only the things that matter to you and your purpose in life. It is huge, and no one can ever know everything in it. There are things that are hidden from your eyes that matter, but there are worlds that we can also explore in a way that no one has ever done before.

So many human beings think that in their logical mind, they can know it all. But none of this makes any sense under analysis. Those who approach life logically will never get their answers. Instead, you must let the answers flow through you and allow the aha moments to come your way.

Many people who have had a near-death experience returned to report that before they crossed over through the veil, they saw their entire life flash before their eyes. This does indeed happen, revealing those significant events that helped us get to where we are now. Whether it is meeting certain people, learning tough lessons, or taking a path less trodden—all of these life events aid us in preparing for our rebirth in the Afterlife.

In the next stage of your healing journey in the Afterlife, you'll move on from the Waiting Room to the Viewing Room, taking your Life Contract with you to complete your Life Review, which is one of the most difficult but rewarding processes on your journey of healing.

CHAPTER 11

LIFE REVIEW:
THE VIEWING ROOM

During a meditation, Josiah the Elder explained to me how the next stage of the healing journey begins:

> *After checking in and being given your Life Contract, you are escorted to the next step along the healing journey, the Viewing Room. Here, you will conduct a Life Review by witnessing the important events of your last incarnation.*
>
> *Upon arrival, you will be seated in the middle of a circle and surrounded by members of your team, who hold hands and project their energy toward you. It is a very beautiful sight. Imagine yourself in the center of such a gathering, with all of the souls and helpers from all of your lifetimes focused on your healing with their spiritual energy.*

As Josiah described the welcoming scene that greets souls entering the Viewing Room to me, I was able to see it in vivid detail. Whenever I'm given such a rich vision of the Afterlife, I wish that I could somehow project the image that's in my head onto a large screen for all to see. There are no words to describe the beauty and intensity of what I was shown, but I will do my best. . . .

In the Viewing Room, spirit helpers appear to be arranged in a circle, looking like bright 3-D lightbulbs, radiating energy out beyond their fuzzy edges to connect with each other and form a ring of light. The newly arrived soul sits in the middle of that ring, surrounded by a team that has but one purpose: to lend its powerful energy to heal that soul.

It can be overwhelming for a soul to experience so much energy and support. As I've mentioned, all sensation and emotion in the Afterlife is heightened, so the energy around the soul is powerfully intense, something that could never be possible on Earth. Try to imagine a powerhouse of electricity running through all the souls in the room, filling them with a light so brilliant that it's almost blinding to the human eye. Now imagine throwing a switch to intensify that electric energy a hundredfold to get an idea of what it's like.

If a soul felt in any way depleted from its time in the Waiting Room or from its travels around the Earth plane that preceded this stage, here that soul is given the strength to accomplish the next healing step: the Life Review.

The Life Review

When you're in the Afterlife, you'll be taken from the welcoming circle I just described and brought into a theater area that's central to the Viewing Room, in order to begin a review of your latest incarnation. The Life Review is one of the most challenging processes you'll go through on the other side, but it is perhaps the most crucial. Here you must face the unresolved issues you created in the life you just left, feeling deeply the pain of those issues and accepting your part in bringing them about.

One reason why this experience is so difficult is because at this early stage you still have an ego, unlike those more evolved souls who have transformed every aspect of themselves into pure energy and have no need for an ego. Some souls do choose not to follow the route advised by their guides, retaining strong egos even though they've been in the Afterlife for a while. Yet for those who follow the healing pathway as directed, all ego will be stripped away to allow true healing and growth to begin.

Some souls have already begun the process of losing their egos before arriving in the Viewing Room, possibly when they took their first trip back to the Earth plane. There, they witnessed their wrongdoings and failures, and learned what people actually thought of them. They also saw how much they were loved—and while this can have the opposite effect and boost the ego, generally it does not. For many, the ego must be put aside for them to feel vulnerable and accept love.

Getting back to the Life Review, know that as you go through it, your guides will give you the strength and courage you need. All members of your team have been assigned a task correlating to the strengths of their soul and the lessons they themselves have learned. Because of this specialization, you'll find that during different processes of your learning, you become closer to some guides than others. Your master guide will be with you as you do your Life Review, but that spirit's role becomes less central at this stage. Now your master guide takes more of an oversight role and steps in only to offer added support when needed to boost your healing.

Of course, you will never be left alone during your sojourn in the Afterlife. Between healing stages, you share much time and energy with your master guide, having fun and enjoying each other's company. You'll reminisce about the times you had together, both in the life that you just left and in the times you had between lives. Your soul mate, if he or she is in the Afterlife, will be watching your Life Review with you as well, but cannot help you complete this process. There will be plenty of time to be with him or her after your journey is done.

Ben explains what it's like to do your Life Review:

> *You view every aspect of your life: the good, the bad, and the ugly. The words you have said, the gifts you have given, the things and people you have embraced, and the way you have lived. In the Viewing Room, it will all leap up before your eyes. This is not an easy process, as you will see the hurt that you caused and the pain that you suffered. You experience it all again, but this time you are looking at it from the perspective of others. You are able to assess the conflicts in terms of how your actions hurt others. And you experience their pain.*

In the Life Review, you are going to look at your life as a whole, facing everything from beginning to end. You'll see the impact you had on people and that which they had on you, and you'll look at the way you dealt with situations or failed to deal with them. But the most difficult thing you'll have to do is feel the hurt and pain you caused other people. On Earth you didn't do this, since you lived from your own perspective and never truly knew how what you did affected others. Now you see your lessons from the perspective of those who suffered as a result of your words and actions. It's hard . . . and if this process isn't an incentive to treat everyone with love and respect on the Earth plane, then I don't know what is!

Witnessing Your Life

In the Viewing Room, you witness the events of your life projected on many different walls, as if you were in a cinema with multiple screens. Yet the interior of this room is set up to provide you with an experience of maximum intensity, greater than any movie theater on Earth. As Ben describes:

> So circular and grand, the Viewing Room is almost off-putting. Think of the most grand hotel imaginable, and then double that in stature. It is almost too grand for words. There are what you would consider to be marble structures—but remember, we do not have the material substances you have in your world, so I am describing it in terms you can understand.
>
> The main room has a domelike ceiling that is inscribed with bold paintings and drawings, all very beautiful and peaceful. There are gold trimmings everywhere, and a huge dial in the middle of the room that moves as different aspects of your life are projected for review.
>
> All around the room, screens are positioned on walls to display the many different projected memories of your life. Pillars separate these walls, creating sections for screens that are smaller or larger, depending on the event you are witnessing. Some sections contain multiple screens, allowing you to see

how an event occurred in your mind—and then, on an adjacent screen, how that same event played out for another person. And on other screens, you will see scenes of how others felt, so at any time you can have several memories and their associated feelings projected at once.

You and your guides are the only ones in the Viewing Room, but there are other souls who are waiting for their turn. During this process, you do not sit but stand; you are not there to relax and observe your life passively. You are there to actively witness the events you have endured and the impact your actions have had on the lives of others.

In a meditation, I received more information about what happens in the Viewing Room from Josiah the Elder:

As you look at your life there, you will understand the lessons you had, your accomplishments, and how you were able to achieve them. You will also see the tasks that you should have completed but did not. Using a checklist from your original contract, it is your job to see the tasks and lessons you did or did not achieve. You will also see the pain and suffering you caused, and the joy and happiness you created with each individual person.

You see, the point of coming to Earth and being in a body is to learn. Yes, we could all live in the spirit realm forever, but we are highly evolved beings who have been given a planet and a universe, so why not live in it?

This process is one of the hardest things that you have ever had to do. It is normal for it to be long, taking three to four weeks in earthly time, if done consistently. But it is actually not very long in <u>our</u> time, taking only about an hour or two for the entire process.

While you're in the Viewing Room, you'll have the chance to stop each memory you're viewing, focus on it, and deeply feel the emotion associated with it. You'll be able to embrace the moment for what it is, handling each one individually. This is *your* process, and you can cope with it in any way you like. Some souls decide to view their entire life first and then rerun it—stopping after certain sections to deal with whatever feelings of love, joy, pain, and suffering come up. Your team will be available to help you through this process if you need it, but you initially have to approach your Life Review yourself.

Once, a spirit who was going through his Life Review came through in a reading I did because he'd just witnessed some of the negative things he'd done on Earth and wanted to apologize and make amends. It was such a lovely experience, one I will never forget.

The reading was for a young girl whose father, Bill, had passed very quickly as the result of a heart attack. When Bill came through, he told his daughter that although he loved her dearly, he knew he hadn't been the best of fathers and had upset many in the family. He explained that reviewing his life was the hardest thing he'd ever had to do. But having realized his mistakes, he wanted to give each of those disgruntled family members a sign that he was sorry.

The sign he was offering was a dollar bill that would appear to them along the road. I thought this was strange, since normally spirits leave a penny for loved ones to find, but I learned that a dollar bill was significant to this man because of its association with his name—*Bill*. His daughter said that she'd be sure to let everyone in the family know that the dollar bill was important and to watch out for it.

Over the next four weeks, each family member whom this man had hurt in life came forward and told Bill's daughter that they had found a dollar on the side of the road and had picked it up, knowing it was from him.

When his daughter returned for another reading, Bill came through again. He was happy that his message had gotten through with her help and that he'd been able to apologize to the individuals he'd wanted to reach. Since then, he realized that he'd upset many other people in his life—so he sent them all a sign of apology, too, this time using the appearance or symbol of a butterfly to signal them. Coming through this second time, Bill said that he finally felt at peace and was satisfied with the connections he'd made with all those he loved.

Note that *everyone* who crosses over is taken to the Viewing Room for a Life Review, including those who were unable to enter into the Afterlife through the pure White Light. For these souls, the choices are fewer as to how they progress through their Life Review, and the process is more intense due to the degree of harm they caused. They'll have to witness the pain and suffering they inflicted on others, as well as the impact their deeds had on everyone surrounding them—and they'll have to feel the intensity of it nakedly, without any resistance. The healing for these souls involves confronting and resolving the issues that compelled them to do the harm they did.

The soul of Adolf Hitler would fit into this category. We all know how Hitler inflicted terrible suffering on millions of people, and how the ripple effect is still touching lives today. Hitler's Life Review, therefore, would consist of feeling and understanding the events he caused and how they affected others. Now it's important to note that because he does not have a physical body, he would not physically feel the pain, but he *would* feel the emotional pain and suffering that he has created. He'd remain in the Viewing Room for a longer period than most, required to feel every emotion his victims felt, with no option to take time off—and then he'd have to seek forgiveness for his wrongdoings. But his journey wouldn't end there, because at some point he'd have to return to the Earth plane and create harmony within his soul.

I've mentioned previously that hell is a state of mind rather than a location in the Afterlife. An extended stay in the Viewing Room, which would be required of a soul who committed wrongs on a scale as large as Hitler's, might seem like hell to some, but it is not. As difficult as the process might be, the Life Review for such a soul is still a healing one, not a condemnation or sentence of eternal suffering. Once these types of souls have gone through this process, they can work on themselves in the Afterlife or as human beings in the next lifetime, continuing to get life lessons and grow so that next time they can make it to the Afterlife through the pure White Light.

I cannot repeat this often enough: Hell is a state of mind that we trap ourselves in. If you think that you're going to go to hell when you pass, then you're going to create a life filled with pain and torment. But again, *there is no hell.* What you witness in the Viewing Room is probably the closest thing to hell you could ever imagine, since experiencing the hurt and suffering you caused other people will be very intense. Think of times in your life when you allowed yourself to feel the pain of having hurt someone you loved, and then imagine this magnified many times. However, only by being so vulnerable and open will you be able to accept, and thus be cleansed of, your harmful actions. When you accept that you put people through such pain, you'll be able to move on in your healing journey.

When Pain Means Growth

While you do focus on the harm you caused other people in the Viewing Room, it is also an opportunity for you to see how your actions contributed to the growth of those individuals. Everyone must go through some pain for his or her own growth—whether it comes in the form of divorce, financial ruin, abuse, addiction, or just life's disappointments—and sometimes you are the conduit for such experiences to befall others. The story of a reading I did will help explain this, showing how your part in the suffering of others can lead them to greater healing and advancement in their evolution . . . and do the same for you as well.

Marina came to me to explore where her life was going, and to see if she was on the right path. She said that she didn't require my services as a medium, but preferred a psychic reading. While I always try to comply with a client's request, I can't always determine if a spirit is going to want to visit from the other side; if it does, of course, I will not stop it.

During the reading, information came through that shed some light on Marina's marriage to a man she'd then divorced. Her guide was showing me that my client had been stuck in a rut in this marriage of ten years, and leaving had helped her get around the negative blocks in her own life that were causing stagnation in the relationship. She was able to move on, meet the man of her dreams, and start her life again. Marina needed a lot of change and stimulation, and her new partner was very similar to her in that way. He'd taught her some key lessons in life in the short time they'd been together, and she'd already matured and grown in many ways.

When I told Marina that I felt the presence of a male figure, and we determined that it was her ex-husband, she was moved and started to tear up. Her ex had died suddenly about two years after their relationship had ended, and she'd felt guilty, as if the divorce had contributed to his passing.

During the reading, Marina's ex-husband told her that when they separated, he hadn't wanted to accept that the marriage was over and he'd have to move on with his life. He had remained very angry and hurt and tried to hold on to her in whatever way he could. However, with the wisdom he'd gained on the other side, he understood why he'd gone through the painful breakup. He came to see how negative he'd been in the relationship, and that his behavior was something *he* needed to be responsible for, not blame Marina or anyone else for. If Marina hadn't divorced him, he wouldn't have gotten the opportunity to learn this lesson, which included apologizing and asking for forgiveness. In life, he could never do that, but now he was fulfilling his Life Contract and gaining the insight he needed in the Afterlife.

As a soul undergoing your Life Review, you'll discover that even though you may have hurt someone, the pain impacted that person's life and allowed him or her to grow from it. Imagine being in a destructive relationship, and even though you want to leave, you don't—the person you're with is begging you to stay, and it's easier to just do that and not go out in the world to start dating again. But by not taking action, you're only putting your happiness on hold, as well as the other person's growth. So often, when you do hurt others for their own good, you help them grow. They learn from this situation and go on to have a fulfilling relationship as a result of the lessons your relationship taught them.

For example, when Simon, Charlie's dad, and I split up, it was so painful that I didn't think I'd make it through the ordeal. He hurt me immensely, and it took a long time for me to get over the experience. However, we now have a great relationship and are caring parents for our son, and I am very thankful for that.

The suffering I endured helped me find my own personal strength, among other qualities about myself that I now treasure. I had to go through that experience to become the person I am today. It was an amazing learning curve for me, but one that helped me so much. At the soul level, Simon will have to experience that pain himself, but he'll also see how the pain ultimately helped me. In both cases there will be a healing benefit.

Did You Leave Too Soon?

Some souls feel that their lives ended too early and they were taken from the Earth plane before it was their time to leave. As these souls go through their Life Reviews, they may decide that they want to end their time in the Afterlife and return to Earth to reincarnate and heal the wounds they now realize they caused. In this case, they could be born back into their original families (or to those who are close to the families) to impact the lives that need healing. Depending upon the lessons required for the healing, it's also possible that the souls could go elsewhere to reincarnate and experience the same lessons but in different situations.

Even though early returns do happen, they are not advised. The full Life Review is such an integral part of a soul's healing in the Afterlife that if it's cut short, patterns from the soul's last life may be carried over into the next. The Life Review is an opportunity to break a negative cycle of repeatedly causing pain and harm, so completing the process is the only way to do that.

Josiah talks about the decision to return early that's made by some souls in the Viewing Room:

Your lessons are the turning points in your life. In the Viewing Room, you can decide whether you want to experience those turning points or whether you want to stop and analyze why you did certain things. You can also decide if you need to reincarnate to continue with those lessons or not.

Some souls feel so bad for the pain loved ones go through as a result of their passing that they want to go back to help them get over that pain. But few return at this point—most feel that they need to stay in the Viewing Room and heal more fully from the pain of that life.

In the event that a soul does choose to return, it is allowed to do so quickly and given a new situation to learn the lessons it still needs to learn. This is normally done in the case of a child who passed young, or a suicide who wants to ease the suffering of those left behind.

If you continue on to do the full review of your life, you'll most likely come to the realization that you left the Earth plane because it was your time to do so. You completed the lessons you set out to learn in your Life Contract—if you didn't complete them, it's because your earthly body failed or the right situation didn't come along and you missed an opportunity. Regardless, it was still your time to leave, even though there are some things you didn't finish. *Those* life lessons will be there for you to work on in the Afterlife or when you return again to Earth.

For each of us, there is a destined time to leave this dimension. It is written in our Life Contracts, so whenever we depart, it is always the "right time," no matter what the circumstances of our passing or what we believe about it. How you respond to the eventuality of your exit point from the Earth plane—with peace and awareness, or with struggle and resistance—is up to you. But now that you know more about the Afterlife, I hope you'll see that there is nothing you need to resist. This knowledge ought to free you to more fully live your life, without any anxiety that you'll be taken early or have your lifetime here unjustly "cut short."

The Bucket List: Knowing When It's Time to Go

I've heard people talk of having a detailed checklist of what they want to accomplish before they die, called a "bucket list" (referring to the expression "kick the bucket"). On it are the names of people, places, and experiences they want to see or have before passing from earthly life. For these men and women, checking off the items on their bucket list is a way to acknowledge when it's time to pass, which is when they've completed all that they set out to do in life.

I want to share the following stories about a few individuals who had an *idea* of what they wanted to have happen in their lives, but who responded to the *reality* very differently.

Phyllis came to me many years ago because she was afraid to retire. For decades she'd put everything into her career, often to the detriment of her friends and family. Phyllis felt that without her work, she'd have no life, so she sold her business but stayed on to work as a consultant. When she reached age 70, the new company owners insisted that she retire, but she refused. At our meeting, she expressed her anxiety that retirement meant her time in life was up, and she wouldn't be on the Earth plane for much longer.

Phyllis made a list of some places she wanted to see—her bucket list—but she decided to wait before going to any of them. Instead, she set up another business, a smaller one, and kept on working. When she finally passed away at age 90 after selling her second business to a corporation, she had in fact seen a few of the places that were on her list and had some fun along the way. But when her family came to me for a reading, she came through and said something very interesting: that even if she'd given up her business at age 70, when she was first asked to retire, she still would have lived until 90, since that was the age set in her Life Contract for passing.

I now realize that I missed out on so many things, Phyllis revealed. *I managed to learn my lessons in a different way, although I didn't have as much fun as I might have had.* Too late, Phyllis discovered that she could have retired early and accepted that her time to leave was already arranged, and then enjoyed her final years more fully.

I had a very different encounter with a husband and wife who, unlike Phyllis, embraced life to the fullest and lived out their bucket list of dreams to the very end.

Jean and Mike had been together on the Earth plane as soul mates and were incredibly devoted to each other. They met at school, married, and had two beautiful daughters whom they adored. They worked hard all their lives and gave their children everything, including a beautiful home and what some would say was the perfect life. Unfortunately, the couple passed in a fatal car accident far from home, and their daughter Melissa came to see me to get some answers.

As soon as I sat down with Melissa, I felt a surge of overwhelming love coming from the other side. I never ask clients to give me any information about themselves or their life before the reading or even why they've come to see me, so I had no clue as to what was coming through. I simply told Melissa that she was getting so much love from Spirit that it was overpowering. Then I felt the presence of two souls coming forward who wanted to connect with her. I established that it was Melissa's mother and father, and she was so relieved that the weight on her shoulders seemed to lift right away. Jean and Mike started to talk about their life and special memories that they had created as a family. It was a pure connection from them to their daughter, and the love flowed through strongly.

Because Melissa's parents had died with no witnesses, she was seeking some details about their deaths for the sake of closure. The accident had occurred on a quiet road, the car was in good working order, and both of her parents had been careful drivers—so there was no reason for anything to happen. It had been a terrific shock for Melissa and her sister to get a phone call that awful day, saying that both their parents had been killed in a crash.

I learned from Melissa that Jean and Mike had done everything together. When they retired within a month of each other, they decided to take a trip to New Zealand, a place that they'd both planned to visit for years. It took six months to make the preparations because they wanted to savor every moment and make it the trip of a lifetime. For years the two had dreamed of a certain small island off the coast, wanting to watch the sunset together while sitting on the beach. At the end of their three-week vacation, they planned to find this special place as a memorable conclusion to their trip.

When Mike and Jean came through in Melissa's reading, they talked about all the sights they'd seen and the many events they remembered from their trip. They also told me that they'd taken a photo of the sunset from "their" beach, and that it was breath-taking. *Ask her about the picture—she has it*, Jean said to me.

I told Melissa what her mother had said, and Melissa pulled out the photo. It turns out that Jean and Mike had e-mailed it via cell phone to their daughters only minutes before they drove back to their hotel in order to pack for their journey home. This truly lovely photo was their final memory, a sight they'd been waiting to see for much of their lives.

Jean came through to tell Melissa what had happened during their last moments. The sun had gone down, and they were traveling along a dark road. Mike was driving and had remarked that he wasn't feeling very well, attributing it to the stress of flying, which he'd never enjoyed. Suddenly, he slumped over on the steering wheel from a heart attack. At first, Jean didn't know what had happened—her husband seemed to have fallen asleep, and she tried to wake him. In the panic that followed, the car swerved and hit a concrete wall head-on. Both Jean and Mike passed instantly.

Jean continued, saying, *The funny thing is that in that moment of panic, I was overwhelmed by a feeling of utter calmness. I knew that we were both going to be okay. Everything slowed down; and before I knew it, we were both outside the car, looking down at it and at our physical bodies. The car was crushed up against the wall with steam pouring out from under the hood.*

Melissa was in tears at this point, while Jean continued to tell me more. She showed me that in the Life Contract she and Mike had made before coming to the Earth plane, there was an agreement to pass together. Both of Melissa's parents wanted her to know that they were content and happy. They'd learned the lessons they needed to learn, to the best of their earthly ability, so it was their time to leave the Earth plane. There was only one thing they hadn't done on their bucket list, and that was watching the sunset on their special island. Once they'd done so, they were ready to go. And so they did . . . together!

Moving On

As you do your Life Review in the Viewing Room, you'll discover what you learned in this life and what you didn't. Know that you'll continue to work on any unfinished lessons in the next healing stages of the Afterlife, as well as when you return to the Earth plane again.

As you've seen, the purpose of doing the Life Review is to fully embrace and accept everything you've experienced in your lifetime. Once you've looked at this incarnation fully, you're then able to move on. However, you must also remember that throughout your journey of learning and growth in the Afterlife, you're able to come back to the Viewing Room at any time to get the help you need in order to heal.

Ben gives us a hint of what comes next:

> *After the Viewing Room, you move forward to the Healing Room. You are escorted by your guides and also some members of your soul family who have specific roles to play in your healing. Others will be saying their good-byes for a short while, as their assigned work may be done.*

Some souls need more healing than others, and this is something your guides know before you arrive on the other side. They've gathered together with the help of your Elder to ensure that you have everything you need to complete the tasks you'll face. Looking at your life and the suffering you caused others can be overwhelming, but you *will* be able to cope with it—by this stage, you're increasingly thinking as a *spiritual* being, not a *human* being. In addition, you're given much help and guidance and offered much comfort, as I've told you; however, there is also a lot of knowledge I haven't been privy to, since it is sacred knowledge and must remain that way.

Yet you'll be happy to know that your hand will be held every step of the way—and those doing the hand-holding are highly qualified, as they've gone through this exact same process themselves and know what to expect. In addition, they've been assigned to you because of their skills and dedication to helping you heal. But do understand that as well as your guides know the path, their helping you aids their souls in their own growth in the Afterlife, preparing them for the next stage of *their* journey.

As soon as the job of a guide is finished, that spirit will leave you and no longer be on your healing team. This is not a final good-bye; rather, it is a temporary farewell, as you'll see all your guides again in another part of the Afterlife. But for this moment, they must leave you because their work is done.

As I've said, there is always someone helping you, in addition to your master guide who is very much like your best friend, so take comfort that you will never be alone. As Ben assures you:

> *Your guides in the Viewing Room may have helped you look at your Life Contract and enabled you to see your life in a different way. They may have been by your side just for emotional support. They may have been there to help you and guide you or simply to hold your hand, but in either case, they now have other jobs to do. You will see them again, so do not worry.*

Now that you're familiar with the Viewing Room and the Life Review process, it's time to move on to an advanced stage of healing—in the appropriately named Healing Room.

CHAPTER 12

PURE HEALING: THE HEALING ROOM

Continuing on from the Viewing Room, you enter the next stage of your journey in the Healing Room. Here, you'll become engulfed by an energy that will rid you of the last vestiges of pain and trauma that are part of being human. And since you've just reviewed your life, you'll certainly benefit from what is available to you in this room. As Josiah says:

> Some souls head straight to the Healing Room after their time in the Viewing Room; others go forward and backward, visiting loved ones and then the Healing Room. It is in the Healing Room that most souls get over any remaining ill effects they experienced in their transition to the Afterlife.
>
> When you first enter the Healing Room, the vibration is so high and the energy so powerful that you may have a feeling of dizziness or nausea. But once you are pulled into the energy's loving embrace, you find that the room has more to offer, and you will not want to leave.

Developing a Positive Attitude

Before I describe the Healing Room in detail, I want to touch on the importance of attitude as you progress on your journey. Believe it or not, the attitude you bring to your life now is connected to your future incarnations and even your evolution in the Afterlife.

I'm always fascinated when people say, "Well, my problems may be bad, but they aren't as bad as *that* person's." This may be true, and it's certainly a very humble and honorable viewpoint to have. But it's not the problems in life you should compare—it's the attitude you *bring* to those problems that makes the difference.

Have you ever had an experience that was difficult for you to go through but was a walk in the park for someone else? For example, maybe you had a rough time at work because your boss was criticizing your performance. You then handled it the only way you knew how: by becoming stressed and overwhelmed. However, a co-worker with the same boss may have dealt with the same situation very differently, keeping a matter-of-fact attitude and not taking any of it personally.

I saw this phenomenon when I was involved with two people who were diagnosed with cancer. One of them battled the illness heartily, bringing to it a positive, "get this sucker out of my body" attitude. She wasn't going to let the disease win, so she went to work daily while continuing her sessions at the gym. The other person fought her illness in the way she knew how, but her attitude was totally different. She was rather negative, took a weaker stand in the face of the disease, and did little to help herself. She eventually succumbed to the cancer, while the first woman went into remission.

No surprise, you may be thinking, but let's look a little closer. Why should one person live through cancer and another not? Of course, there is a Life Contract already predestining the outcome, but at the same time, we always have free will in how we respond to a situation. As was evident with these two women, bringing an optimistic outlook to a life-threatening situation is one response that can make a great difference.

A positive attitude not only helps you in life, but it follows you into the Afterlife, making your process there go much more smoothly. So if you've suffered from trauma or abuse in this incarnation, don't sweep your pain under the carpet; rather, be willing to face it head-on. Get whatever help you need to understand that it wasn't your fault, and avoid becoming one of life's hopeless victims.

If you can engage in such healing while still on the Earth plane, your soul's journey on the other side will be so much easier. One does relate directly to the other, since the Afterlife is governed by energy—so the thoughts and feelings you bring to your healing process impact your course of evolution instantaneously. As you read further, you'll understand this more fully, but for now, do whatever it takes to put yourself on a path of self-improvement.

The Healing Room

When you reach the Healing Room on the other side, your task is to concentrate on your own healing experience, not to correct any harm you've done or make amends to benefit others, as in the Viewing Room. Your stay in this room is geared toward self-discovery, as you'll be learning more about your actions and relationships on the Earth plane.

Some souls resist visiting the Healing Room, believing that witnessing the pain and suffering of others in their Life Review was enough healing for them. But other souls want to understand why they did what they did, in the hopes that it might deepen their healing process. That certainly can happen here.

Before you reach the Healing Room—just as at all other stages of the healing journey—you can go back to any other room to continue your journey in a cyclical fashion. You can also return for a brief visit to the Earth plane if you want to, but only if your soul truly desires this for deeper self-development. Keep in mind that if your motivation to go back to any room or to Earth is self-ish or petty, you'll find that those opportunities are not offered to you again.

When referring to the Healing Room, Ben channeled the following information:

> The Healing Room is awash in aquamarine light—imagine the color of blue topaz, and then add a sparkling metallic twist. The love that you will experience is incredible, unlike any you have experienced on Earth, but it then intensifies as you receive _our_ unconditional love and the healing that comes from it.

Here, you can go through any aspect of your life you need to—anything that caused you great pain. You can work through any issues you have. Whatever is on your mind that you are carrying the weight of, you need to release before you can move on through the spirit realm and complete your healing journey.

Some stay in the Healing Room for a while, needing to be cured of illnesses or abuse of every kind. They may have to heal from the scars that resulted from self-inflicted wounds. In the Healing Room, all souls take time to recover. You come to terms with your passing from the Earth plane, as well as any pain experienced during your exposure to those life events witnessed in the Viewing Room.

In life, as I've said, it's good to take the time to heal from those situations that cause you pain and trauma. As a result of these types of situations, negative emotions often go unexpressed and get bottled up, turning you into a volcano ready to erupt with the least amount of provocation. As soon as something presses your buttons, you release a flood of emotion, as if a dike had burst and the force of oncoming water could no longer be contained.

It will be easier in the Afterlife if you do the work to resolve your emotional issues on the Earth plane first, because, as I've said, everything is more intense in the Afterlife. But just because you dealt with an issue on Earth, that doesn't mean you won't have to deal with it again in the Afterlife. You will, but it will be easier. Knowing this should be strong motivation to get to work on wounds and scars that have been festering during your life, and not wait until you've passed. You're not going to escape confronting these things, so it's better to do so now than then.

∽

You'll stay in the Healing Room as long as you need to. I know that in our human earthly sense, we can't think of anything worse than taking responsibility for the issues we have, but that's because we tend to avoid facing facts. In the Afterlife, we learn that it's good to examine our lives. It feels very freeing, even enlightening;

it isn't heavy, dragging us down or making us unhappy. The thought of having to face uncomfortable feelings is usually what puts us off—but once we start, we open up and the communication flows, much to our great relief.

My son, Charlie, knows how this works, and even explained it quite clearly to me recently. "Mommy, I don't like it when I *have to* talk to you about feelings," he said. "But when I do, I feel so much better that I never want to stop."

Children have a great way of honestly expressing themselves, while we adults are often reluctant to do so. But as soon as we initiate the process, things start to get resolved and love is present, which is why my son doesn't want to stop sharing his feelings. It's the same in the Afterlife, where energy is at its purest and love flows freely. Emotions come more easily, even though we experience them more intensely. But it does help if we learn to share our feelings and express our emotions when on the Earth plane.

Josiah tells us more about the process we undergo in the Healing Room:

> The Healing Room is a place where most souls choose to go. Some who come here from the Viewing Room stay for a while, others only pop in and out, and still others return more than once. For this, you do not need any guides other than the healers, although your master guide is waiting for you outside.
>
> Imagine a large room vaulted by a huge crystal dome; and fill that space with peace, love, and calmness. Multiply your sense of this by a thousandfold, and you will be close to what it is like in the Healing Room.
>
> In the center of the room is a clear crystal—for your human understanding, say that it is made of quartz rock. Energy is channeled through this area, so it remains contained, moving around in the center. You are seated around the edge of this powerful vortex, positioned so your soul is engulfed by the powerful healing energy the Healing Room has to offer.

Work of the Healers

Healers are exceptional souls whose singular purpose in the Afterlife is to provide you with optimal wellness so that you can take the next step in your journey. They're trained and dedicated to help you, and not just in the Healing Room—they also assist you in overcoming difficult issues in life.

From the channeled message below, which I received from Josiah, we see how healers work closely with us on the Earth plane to speed up the process of healing in the Afterlife:

Those souls who assist in the Healing Room are the healers, but they also work with people on the Earth plane to make sure that a person's physical body is sustained for the time it is there. They also help human beings heal from emotional turbulence and distress.

The human world is not like this one; we do not have the pain and the heartache you do. Therefore, the healers work very closely with you in your dimension so that they can move you through life. But not everyone is willing to embrace such healing; some resist or avoid it. This makes it difficult, since it is crucial that people acknowledge that they are receiving a healing. Souls must accept the healing while still on the Earth plane, so they can be helped to move forward in life with whatever issues they need to resolve.

The healers are all highly evolved souls, some of whom did healing work on the Earth plane when they were still in a body. As a result of their experiences, they've learned many life lessons and are able to share their vast knowledge with you. They'll guide you through everything you need in order to heal from the trauma of your passing, especially if it was from a long illness or a violent death. You are in safe hands.

Josiah tells us more about this work of the healers, and how different souls progress and are helped through the Healing Room:

The healers help you through the grieving process of having transitioned from the Earth plane. Yes, you have to grieve the life that you have left behind. It is normal and very common.

Certain souls can detach from their grief easily, but they are few and far between. They tend to be those who had an abusive upbringing and learned to escape that reality on Earth, or those who have led a spiritual life and gotten a taste of the process we go through in the Afterlife.

Those who come to the Healing Room stay for various lengths of time, depending on the soul and how it passed from the body. Someone who passed suddenly or violently may stay longer, for instance. But those who endured the physical pain that accompanies diseases such as cancer may not stay long, since they often had time to come to terms with their passing.

Some souls who had cancer might stay for a longer time, though, if their disease was so bad that they could not cope and suffered terribly. There are also those who had long-term illnesses, such as dementia or Alzheimer's, who need to heal extensively from the pain that their illness caused. Some were afflicted by other mental-health issues and could not express themselves in their efforts to resolve issues, so they need to heal deeply from the pain of their life.

Each case is unique; but as you recall, all souls have their own time to go back and visit their loved ones, accomplishing a level of healing that permits them in the Viewing Room to take in the pain and the suffering that they caused. They are then ready for the Healing Room.

The exceptions are those troubled souls who did not make it through the pure White Light, but entered the Afterlife through a different light portal. They have their own room for healing, which is very similar to, but not the same as, this Healing Room. That is to say, they are kept separate. Only when they have learned their lessons and are ready to be integrated back do they head to the pure White Light of love to join the others on their final path.

It is a very difficult process for these souls, and we try to help them as much as we possibly can. Eventually, they come back through the Viewing Room and then head to the Healing Room, so they are constantly being healed throughout their journey. But even after they have gone through both rooms, they never enter the higher levels in the Afterlife, as do other souls. However, at every step, they are embraced with love and never judged by us in the way that human forms have judged them.

After the Healing Room, they skip the stages of the healing journey that most souls go through and head directly to a room where they are prepared to enter earthly life. Three different sets of parents are chosen for them, and they choose which of these they will be born to. The process is fast, and they return to the Earth plane very quickly to continue working on their lessons. Most souls, however, stay longer to work through the more advanced realms of the soul world.

Healing Chambers

Josiah's description of what a soul experiences upon first entering the Healing Room is very beautiful and inspiring. However, during the meditations I've had while writing this book, I've come to know about several smaller chambers within the vast Healing Room, and each of them is unique.

I've been given some information about these smaller rooms by Ben, but even though I've been on this journey for some time with my guides and have knowledge from Spirit, I'm not privy to everything there is to know. There are big chunks of the Afterlife I'm not able to share with you, for much sacred knowledge is held there. One thing I can assure you of is that you'll experience a tremendous amount of love throughout every stage of your sojourn in the Afterlife.

Here is Ben's description of the first of the smaller healing chambers within the Healing Room:

There are many different chambers or sections within the greater Healing Room. One of these is the Yellow Room, where you go to heal from illnesses you took on as a physical body but that also had an impact on your soul. This room is filled with the brightest yellow there is, and in it you are completely suffused by the warm brilliance of a sun that fills you and the healers who work with you with loving energy.

Bodily disease is often created by other people's dark energy in life, or by harmful situations you're in. You may have held your own negative emotions in for so long that your body became impacted, so you must be healed from this. In the Yellow Room, you only deal with the impact that a disease has left on you, not why the disease came about. Sometimes that illness was called for in your Life Contract, but it still left an impact on your soul and thus needs to be addressed.

Some people become ill for a reason, and that was true for me. I had to fight cancer and undergo a hysterectomy when I was quite young, all so I could develop compassion and empathy for those who can't have children and those who fight life-threatening diseases. I also learned to maintain a positive attitude that I could overcome my conditions, no matter how hard they were to bear. Having gone through all of this, while incredibly painful, has made me stronger to face other challenges in life.

Ben continues:

The Green Room is for those souls who in life had mental illnesses, such as the many forms of dementia; as well as depression, birth defects, schizophrenia, and others. They are here to overcome why they had these issues and what the reasons were for them. It is difficult to be in the room because there has been so much suffering. Often when souls have been healed from these issues, they move on to the Pink Room to deal with related issues.

The Pink Room is focused on healing from abuse. This is where you go through a process of self-discovery to realize that you were not the abuser, but rather were the one who had to deal with the abuse.

This last message needs clarifying, since the topic of abuse is a very sensitive one, as well as something so many people misunderstand. Those who were abused as children—whether verbally, physically, or sexually—often believe that they were responsible for the abuse, because that's what they were told for so long by the adults involved. But this is not correct. If you suffered abuse as a child—especially sexual abuse—you were the victim, not the abuser, and this is very important to realize.

I've done several readings in which I've seen that the victims of abuse themselves became abusers because it's all they knew . . . particularly if they didn't realize what was going on and failed to understand it correctly. For instance, if someone was emotionally abused as a child, that individual probably grew up thinking that such behavior was acceptable to others. Then, because of this programming, the abusive behavior became a pattern that was repeated later in life with his or her own child. In readings, I've seen family members realize how abuse came about and receive closure from understanding it.

More from Ben:

There is also the Red Room, which is where those who have given much pain to others are sent. There, they must go through the reasons why they did what they did, and then they have to look at their lives. Only then can they move through the process and into the other rooms.

Finally, there is the Amethyst Room, a very beautiful and peaceful place that is bathed in purple light. This is where the majority of your time in the Healing Room is spent. When you arrive here, you have most likely already spent some time in the other rooms. In the Amethyst Room, you get rid of the last amounts of pain and suffering you brought with you from the Earth plane, actually wiping the slate clean and freeing yourself to move forward.

∽

The Healing Room is an area for self-discovery as well as healing. After your time there, you have the choice to either stay on in the Afterlife or return to the Earth plane and go through your lessons again.

From what Spirit has communicated about the healing journey in the Afterlife, it seems that you'll be given every opportunity to heal the wounds that have followed you there from the Earth plane. It's clear that if you don't spend enough time on the other side working on your issues, old patterns of harm and suffering will be perpetuated when you incarnate again. Therefore, as you journey through the Afterlife, it's important to experience every stage to help your soul heal and become stronger, so that eventually you'll be free to move on to what awaits you beyond.

I will tell you exactly what is waiting for you . . . right after we visit the last room of the journey.

CHAPTER 13

THE SOUL'S GREATER POWER: THE GUARDIANSHIP ROOM

Your healing journey in the Afterlife has taken you through the Meeting Room, the Waiting Room, the Viewing Room, and the Healing Room; and now it is almost complete. The last room you enter will reconnect you with your spirit guides and help you discover the best path for your continuing evolution as a soul. (As in all stages of your journey, you can return to any of the aforementioned rooms for more healing before you move on.)

Think of your visit to the Guardianship Room as career counseling; that is, an opportunity to assess your strengths and weaknesses and choose the work you'll do in the future. After you do so, you'll be free to explore the wider environs of the Afterlife, undertaking lessons and tasks that move you up the celestial hierarchy and eventually prepare you to reincarnate back on Earth. In the words of Josiah:

> *Once through the Healing Room, you move on and arrive at the Guardianship Room. There, you and your master spirit guide review your progress so far, discussing the help you were offered and whether or not you took it, along with the ways you have changed. As a result of this process, you will become more deeply connected to your guide, enjoying each other's company, and laughing and having fun in the Guardianship Room.*

You will also be shown your Akashic Record, which details your entire existence—including your time in the Afterlife as well as all the lives you have ever lived on the Earth plane— and you will be let in on many of the mysteries of life. Then it will be time to discover your next step and make a plan for your remaining time in the realm of Spirit.

Certain raw emotions may have come up from the processes you underwent in the Viewing or Healing Rooms, but now you can deal with the situations that *caused* those emotions—and your growth. This is how cyclical development occurs in the Afterlife, always making opportunities available for deeper healing.

Your arrival in the Guardianship Room marks a kind of graduation, a time of completing the first phase of your learning and healing on the other side. Even though you'll always be gaining wisdom and experiencing growth throughout your existence, your time in the Guardianship Room will prepare you for the path you're going to take as a fully participating citizen of the Afterlife.

Changing Relationships

Before I explain the Guardianship Room in detail, I would like to take a brief detour and talk about the connection you still have with the Earth plane, and how it has changed as you've gone through the Afterlife.

By this point on your healing journey, you're more comfortable with having passed from life, and you've accepted the great voyage you're on. Yet the more you become accustomed to being on the other side, the weaker your bonds with loved ones back on Earth become. As time has passed, it's gotten to the point where they no longer sense your presence in their lives. Having said that, you can still pay them a visit.

As a soul, you're able to hear when an earthbound loved one is thinking of you or calling out for your assistance. You may find that a family member requires your help to fully grieve your passing, for instance, or to go through a particularly difficult situation at work or in a relationship. When you get "the call" from someone on Earth who needs you, you'll want to respond with some kind of message, letting that person know that he or she is not alone and you are nearby. You may have a special sign to indicate your presence, perhaps a piece of music playing at a meaningful time, a butterfly gliding by in nature, or something else you would consider appropriate for that individual.

You might even choose to return and follow a loved one through the day—wanting to establish your presence with your father, son, or brother, perhaps. In that case, he'll know that you're there, often looking behind him and sensing your presence. When you see him do this, you'll want to engulf him with all the love you're experiencing on the other side, expanding your energy out to cover his physical form and fill his aura. This may seem like a warm embrace or hug for you, but it will feel icy cold to your loved one, giving him a shudder or the chills.

You could also feel that the person you want to contact—maybe your mother, daughter, or sister—needs more than the signs you've already given to establish your presence. If so, you can visit her in dreams and connect deeply with her soul. To do so, you'll have to lower your vibrational energy to meet her close to the veil, and she'll have to raise her vibrational energy to meet you.

Meanwhile, Back on the Earth Plane

Back here on Earth, we raise our vibrations naturally whenever we begin to fall asleep. As we drift in and out of consciousness, allowing our subconscious mind to take over, our vibrations accelerate, no longer constrained by our daily concerns. We can then leave our bodies and astral-travel, giving our bodies a chance to relax and heal from any stress or suffering we may have experienced during the day.

Earlier in the book I mentioned my own experience with this phenomenon as a child, in which I would jolt awake in my bed, my conscious mind kicking in to stop me from leaving my body. You, too, may experience this, if you don't feel comfortable enough to astral-travel for whatever reason.

Most people don't remember their travels, but you might wake up and recall a particular man or woman who appeared in your dream, someone whom you know. If this happens, contact that individual and find out if he or she had a dream similar to yours. If you get a positive answer, then you'll know that you and that person were connecting in your dreams and astral-traveling together as you both slept.

When you travel in your sleep, still tethered by the silver cord, you come close to the veil that separates this world from the next. Consequently, you may wake up after such an experience and recall a magic moment with a departed loved one from your dream. Maybe you received visions and messages from him or her, which are very real signs that this soul was trying to get through to you. Or, using the same ability to create a vision, your departed loved ones might project vivid and meaningful memories into your dreams to give you a sign of their presence. They've retained certain details of events you shared with them, since they haven't yet severed their earthly ties entirely.

However, keep in mind that when a soul appears to you in a vision or a dream, it may not look like your memory of the person. When my grandfather comes through, for instance, he is never bald. In life, he was not happy to lose his hair, so now he comes through looking much younger, and with a full head of hair! It took me a while to understand this, but the explanation is simple: since souls have no physical body, they can conjure up any image of themselves they wish—hopefully one you're able to recognize!

Ariel explains how souls' identifying characteristics change in the Afterlife:

As souls stay here longer, the earthly tag of their given name drops away. When we return to Spirit, we all receive back the name that was given to us from our many sojourns here. For example, my name here is Ariel, but my tag on the Earth plane was Margaret. I was a female, married to a good husband and the mother of five children. Over the period of time that I have been here, however, I have lost my earthly tag. Nor do I still have a sex or gender, as you would put it. My energies are feminine, which is why you have associated me with being a woman. If I decide to incarnate again, I could return as a female or a male, but that is a decision I can make when I am ready.

Seeking Answers from Beyond

It takes a great amount of energy for souls to approach and cross the veil, so don't expect visits to happen very often. In fact, you must come to terms with increasingly fewer visits as time goes on, as the earthly ties of your departed loved ones grow weaker.

In fact, there comes a time in your loved ones' healing journeys when you may hardly feel their presence around at all. It's normal for this to happen, but not because they've forgotten about you. Instead, departed souls know when they're needed and when it's best to visit, getting that information directly from listening to us on the Earth plane.

It's important to understand that souls in the Afterlife see you in a different light than you see yourself. They rely on information from your aura, or energetic body. Since your aura is a direct source of energy, it will never lie, so your departed loved ones can know what is truly needed at any time. Souls can tell from your aura where you are in your grieving process, and whether it would be beneficial for you to have a visitation or not. (You may not understand why it wouldn't be a good idea for a soul to see you; but trust me, as a medium, I know how a visit might adversely affect you.)

The truthful information in your aura is also what allows people who are empathic to know things you may have thought no one would ever know. Thankfully, there are ways of shutting down this ability, which can be necessary as you go about your daily life. In my case, for example, I don't go around all day talking to dead people—there is a time and a place for that. Because I've learned to focus and manage my energy, most souls I encounter respect my boundaries and don't hound me to get their messages across, unless it's about something urgent, and then I make myself available.

Thanks to the knowledge from your aura that souls in the Afterlife are privy to, they know you better than you know yourself. That's why before I give someone a reading, I always ask, "Do you want to know everything?" I need permission before I relate all that a spirit is telling me.

Understand that you are always connected to Source; your departed loved ones know that and only tell you what is necessary for your growth. Some information they communicate to you will be difficult, but you'll never be given anything you cannot handle. Also, a spirit won't tell you *everything* you're going to encounter in life—there are experiences you must go through without foreknowledge so that you can learn a crucial lesson or discover something important about yourself.

If a soul needs to get a message to you, it will likely lead you to the right person who will convey that information to you. You may randomly meet an individual who does readings, or someone will recommend a medium to you . . . but know that there are *no* coincidences in life, and something that appears random is actually not. This is something we all come to realize as we move through our life's journey.

∽

Whenever someone makes contact with a departed loved one, it can be tempting to keep the communication going through repeated readings. However, this can be unhealthy for both the person seeking messages and the soul being called upon. Frequent visits can actually hinder clients, creating a dependence on souls for guidance to the extent that they no longer make their own decisions. Of course, as I've said, souls in the Afterlife can monitor their loved ones' progress, and will only give them as much connection as is needed.

I'm reminded of a client I had in the U.K. named Chloe. This woman came to me because she had lost her husband and had unfinished business with him. He'd taken his own life, leaving her to run his company and handle his many other affairs. She was very angry with her husband, but found that she couldn't make important decisions without seeking his advice.

The first time I read for Chloe, she got the answers she wanted, including the business advice she needed to carry on. When she came back to see me later in the year, I didn't find this to be a problem at all. Happily, her husband came through again—but this time, having healed from whatever was troubling him on the Earth plane, he was back to being the soul Chloe had fallen in love with. Their bond was very strong.

For our next few readings, Chloe developed the habit of regularly booking a session with me right after we finished our current one. At the time, I had a waiting list of six months, so I was comfortable setting her up with an appointment that wasn't too close to the last one. However, as the time between sessions grew shorter, I began to suspect that my client's frequent contact with her husband might not be so healthy.

Finally, Chloe's husband communicated to me that he wasn't able to continue coming through in our readings anymore, since it was holding up his process by keeping him tied to our dimension. It was hard for me to convey to Chloe what her husband had said, particularly since she did *not* want to hear it. Furthermore, unbeknownst to me, she was getting readings from other mediums in between her readings with me.

The next time Chloe came to see me, her husband didn't show up. Instead, her spirit guide came forward to tell her to stop having readings and allow life to take its natural course. Chloe's guide revealed that it was written in her Life Contract that her husband would commit suicide, but she'd get over it and eventually move on.

After that reading I left for the U.S. and didn't see Chloe again, but I did keep in touch with her via e-mail. Recently, I heard from her that she'd met someone and had started a brand-new life. This woman definitely taught me how people can become dependent on readings to the detriment of their own growth, so I made a new rule that no clients could book appointments with me if they'd had a reading within the previous six months.

Even though your departed loved ones eventually stop giving you regular messages and signs, know that they're still connected to you. They will hear you and be available to you for as long as they can. But they also have to move on through the Afterlife, and being constantly called upon isn't good for their development. Have patience, and know that you will be with them again on the other side.

When Visits Stop

If departed loved ones have stopped visiting you altogether, there could be a simple explanation. Souls can judge by your earthly emotions if it's best to contact you, and then they plan their visits according to what they discover. They may find that their continual visitations are too hard on you, and since they have come to terms with their own passing and are adjusting well to the Afterlife, they choose to move on and focus on their own healing process.

It's also possible that your loved ones have returned to the Earth plane to reincarnate. When this happens, souls will be less available for any kind of communication that involves speaking. As a medium, I've learned that an imprint of the soul's energy is left on the other side, much like DNA traces are left on an article of clothing or fingerprints are left on a glass. A medium can read that imprint but not connect to receive any messages.

If signs or visitations from your departed loved ones have stopped due to their reincarnation and you want to find them in their new bodies, look for individuals with the same eyes as the ones you lost. The eyes are windows to the soul and can give you the clues to whom your loved ones may be this time around. You also need to trust your gut instinct—if you feel that someone you meet is a loved one who has returned, then you should trust that feeling and explore the possibility.

Finally, there are those souls who are so happy and fulfilled in their Afterlife journey that they feel no need to contact you anymore. These souls may continue to check in on you, but they'll no longer leave signs or give you messages, having dissolved their earthly bonds to the extent that you no longer hear from them. They're still connected, if not actively—but you'll notice that you've moved on, too, and may be giving them less thought as the years go by.

The Guardianship Room

Getting back to your journey as a soul, when you visit the Guardianship Room, you reconnect with your spirit guides so that you can discover the path you are to take for the remainder of your stay in the Afterlife. This stage of the journey is so much more relaxing than the intense healing stages you've just gone through—by now, you are at home in the Afterlife and feel quite comfortable.

In the Guardianship Room, you'll have time to catch up with some of the soul connections you haven't seen very much up until now, since you were so busy healing or visiting the Earth plane. During this time, you will deepen your connection with these souls, particularly your master guide. You'll also become better acquainted with the one who's assigned to you as your Elder. As you may recall, Elders are advanced souls whose role it is to check in the newly arriving souls in the Waiting Room and give them their Life Contracts. A soul must advance greatly in its journey to become an Elder; yet although they're highly evolved, Elders still return back to our dimension to help those in need, often becoming spiritual teachers or gurus.

Now is the time for you to reflect on the full meaning of the incarnation you just had, as well as the many lifetimes you had before. In the Guardianship Room, you'll be shown memories of your entire existence in order to determine the significance of events that occurred. You'll discover how your guides have played a part in all of your lives, as well as how you helped your guides in *their* lives. Regarding the mysteries of life, many are revealed, but you'll only be told what you need to know to help you plan your continued journey.

You'll also see your Akashic Record, which is the energetic imprint of your soul and everything you've gone through over many lifetimes: the hurt, the pain, the love, and the sorrow. You'll go over this with your master spirit guide, and it will be like catching up with an old friend you haven't seen for years, sharing and reminiscing while paging through a scrapbook or photo album.

It's important to point out that those dark souls who didn't enter the Afterlife through the pure White Light prepare to return to Earth without spending time in the Guardianship Room. Since they aren't going to remain in the Afterlife, they don't need to go through any kind of planning process. Their fate is a quick trip to the Screening Room to select a new family in which to be born and receive further lessons for their healing growth. (All souls actually go through the Screening Room before reincarnating, and I'll describe this area more fully later in the book.)

*

I found out what a soul goes through in the Guardianship Room when one who'd progressed to this stage came through in a reading.

I'd read for Joan several times over the years. When her mother, Patty, passed away from cancer, my client wanted me to connect with her. Patty had actually been a client of my grandmother's, and while in life, she'd been very open to the spirit world. I had no doubt that when Joan came in for this reading, Patty would show up, too.

And she did. Along with the expected chat about the memories she'd kept with her in the Afterlife, Patty shared some information that neither her daughter nor I was expecting. She said that she'd met the most incredible man on the other side who was extremely handsome and wonderful. As they got to know each other, she realized that they'd been lovers in a past life, and that he'd chosen to stay on in the Afterlife during her journey to the Earth plane.

Patty told her daughter that even though she loved her earthly husband, Joan's father, very much, the handsome man turned out to be her guide and her soul mate. Interestingly, Joan's father was also in the Afterlife—he and her mother were important soul connections, and they were happy to reconnect with each other after Patty passed.

Celestial Career Counseling

In the Guardianship Room, you'll discover what it is that you as a soul need next, just as you might on Earth if you went to a career counselor to plan your future. You might choose to stay on the other side and be with your soul mate, enjoying further opportunities for growth and development. You could take on a role of service and become trained as a guide yourself, joining the ranks of celestial helpers and perhaps becoming an Elder. Or you may decide that you want to go back to the Earth plane. There are many directions your path can take, the choice of which will be up to you. This stage is about discovering what is right for *your* soul.

As Josiah notes:

> *If you have not already returned to the Earth plane and reincarnated, at this stage you will explore your life on the other side. You will be given the opportunity to select a goal, but you are not asked to make a choice yet. It is very much like what you do when considering a career in life.*
>
> *You may find at this time that some of your guides leave you because it is their turn to reincarnate or to move on and help someone else. Guides may ask you to assist them with their next assignment, or request that you be a guide to them. If this is the case, you have an opportunity to see and experience being a guide for another from this point of view.*

You may realize that it's better for your own higher soul development to stay longer in the Afterlife, learning lessons and taking on work that is of service to other souls. You might decide to become a healer, aid the natural universal energies that help the Earth plane continue to live and breathe, or be someone else's spirit guide. There is no right or wrong choice; it is left entirely up to you after your review in the Guardianship Room. Your guides will give you advice and guidance, but they can't decide for you. It's something your soul will know, and that's what you'll choose.

Another discovery you make in the Guardianship Room concerns the lessons you still need to master in your next life. If you're not incarnating for a while, you have plenty of time before you decide what you must learn next. But it's not an easy decision to make—so when the time comes, you're advised to think carefully about it.

Some souls return more quickly than others to the Earth plane at this point because they may have made a hasty decision to do so, but you shouldn't be so rash. *Carefully* considering what your lessons are and how many of them you've accomplished up until now will help you decide on your next step in the journey.

∽

If you decide to stay in the Afterlife, then you'll be assigned a "job" in the Guardianship Room—that is, a way of helping others while you're choosing your next step. You may not want to hear that you'll have to work when you get to the other side, since you've worked very hard all your life and expect something of a vacation when you pass.

Rest assured that the job you'll be assigned will be nothing like your occupation back on Earth; rather, it will be more like a spiritual undertaking in which you'll help others who are on the journey. You may be assigned to welcome a loved one from your own family, just as you were welcomed. You could be given the task of rescuing lost souls who need to cross over into the Light. Or perhaps you'll be sent to help children or animals who are about to pass and need extra support. The list is endless.

You'll be given many opportunities, and these can change with the way you manage your time in the Afterlife. But when it comes to what your assignment is, you won't be given a choice. An Elder will be placed in charge of a greater plan for your soul and will make this choice for you. Even though you do have many choices in accordance with your free will, you still must learn certain lessons in the Afterlife that an Elder will be privy to.

Ariel shares some wisdom on this subject:

> *Your focus is to learn, and you will never stop learning. I have seen so many souls who thought being here was going to be a breeze, but they discover that learning is the hardest part. Then on top of that, we have to tell them they have a job to do! Some are shocked; others accept it; but for all, it is difficult. You have worked all your life, and now when you come back home to a place of peace and tranquility . . . you have to work again.*
>
> *The work you are assigned is different from what you did on the Earth plane. Here, your assignment depends on the lessons you learned in life. The more advanced you are in your soul development, the more important the job is that you are given. All the work is important, of course, but a role is given to you dependent on what you have achieved in terms of your soul's growth.*
>
> *Embrace it and allow it to happen. Your work will prepare you for your next goal in life. That could be helping others pass, working as a spirit guide, or returning back to the Earth plane. Whatever assignment you are given, do it well, and you will move up through the celestial levels—where, eventually, you will reach a state of everlasting being.*
>
> *Of course, your life on the other side will not be all work. There is fun time and laughter, too. There is never any hostility, not how you know it. Instead, the Afterlife is a place of learning and guidance, where you are helped and educated. If you want to head back to the Earth plane to check in on your loved ones, then you can do so. It is a choice, and one that you are allowed to make—although be mindful that it does take a lot of energy, and you may want to conserve that energy for the tasks at hand.*

Exploring the Afterlife

If you choose to stay in the Afterlife, it will be a time to learn, grow, and fully understand the wealth of knowledge you have at your disposal. This includes meeting with your Elder and master guide, if they're still with you at this point. You'll have to continue to check in and make sure that you're achieving the goals you set, but you'll be given plenty of opportunities to move about and discover the wonders of the other side.

Josiah explains:

After your time in the Guardianship Room, you are free to roam around the Afterlife. You are still with your soul connections, whose job is to help keep you on track—this place can be quite entertaining, and some souls go off and do not return for their assignments. When this happens, they stop growing, signaling that it is their time to return to the Earth plane and learn the lessons they need to. On Earth, they will repeat the same patterns they had in their last life in order to once again learn their lessons.

As a soul exploring the other side, you are required to check back in regularly with your Elder and your spirit guide. In your world, this would need to happen weekly, but in our time, it is every half hour. Trust me, though, you will have plenty of time to discover the many incredible places and things that are here.

There is no specific time frame for exploring the Afterlife, as each soul is different, so you can be there as long as your contract calls for. There is so much to be discovered and created in this next stage of the journey, and you have a great deal of free will. Know that the other souls want you to be happy; and you'll be surrounded by peace, love, and tranquility.

This is also the time to focus on your many relationships with your spiritual family. You have a chance to connect more deeply with your soul mate and be at one with him or her, fully experiencing the love you have for one another. And it's a time for you to be with your soul connections and understand why you all are related as a group. Together, you can work for a higher purpose, such as helping create a world of peace. You're also able to visit your loved ones on the Earth plane, but you'll find that such visits are quite rare. Your life is now on the other side, exploring its many dimensions, and you'll be doing so until it become your time to return and incarnate once again.

∽

Before you leave the Guardianship Room, you set those tasks and lessons in the Afterlife that you need to work on. You also have your assignment to fulfill, which may consist of greeting a person from the Earth plane, assisting and guiding that individual on his or her journey of the Afterlife. Your assigned tasks are rewarding and will help you make the most of your time; in fact, the more you work on developing, nurturing, and loving your own soul, the more enlightened you'll become.

Your spirit guide or Elder might ask you to help in a situation you know well from your experience on the Earth plane. Perhaps there's an issue that they're dealing with involving how someone is running his or her life, and they need your knowledge of this dimension to influence it. You may be assigned to help the person being worked with, as the issue could be something you experienced in your earthly life. The issue might be related to complex issues such as greed and materialism, for instance, and if the guide and Elder haven't been back to the Earth plane too recently, they may not understand and will need some help.

Such tasks could be brief, but you'll be expected to take them on—and understand and appreciate them as well—for your own growth. Josiah explains the importance of a soul completing an assignment:

> *You may be assigned to guide or watch over someone who is like you in your last life so you can see the impact you had on others by observing him or her. At the same time, you are there to help that person and his or her guides. In the process, you will see how frustrating it can be when those on the Earth plane*

don't listen to their own inner voice—the very voice that we, as their guides, are sending them.

You can shed fresh light on the situation, showing us why this individual is not listening to us. You have been on the Earth plane more recently than we have, so you can help us broaden our understanding.

Whatever your assignment, it is for the higher good of the universe as well as yourself, and the assignments are changed regularly. This way, when it is your time to return, you will incarnate with a wealth of knowledge enabling you to lead a more spiritually fulfilling life. You will also be able to help those on Earth more if you have accomplished many tasks.

Josiah concludes with a personal note for me:

This is what you did after your last life, in which you committed suicide. You vowed to take on as many tasks and jobs as you could to help people who hurt as much as you did, in order to evolve as a soul.

In spite of all the tasks you're assigned in the Afterlife, you do get plenty of time to relax and enjoy what it has to offer. It's as gorgeous a place as you could ever imagine. There are spectacular places to discover—lakes, streams, and mountain vistas that words cannot describe. Although everything you see is stunningly vibrant, this is also a place filled with peace, love, and harmony.

Josiah attempts to give us a vision:

Oh, this place is so beautiful. Of course, it is all created with the mind and thought, giving a picture of how we want it to look. But it is picturesque and peaceful and brimming with love everywhere.

Materialism and the Afterlife

In spite of the Afterlife's beauty, some souls still have unresolved issues. Thankfully, their issues are never as bad as what people experience in life; it's more like two individuals having a difference of opinion and amicably agreeing to disagree, even laughing about it. That's as bad as it gets! And, of course, these souls are given assignments that are designed to help them resolve their issues.

In some cases, the issues involve materialism and greed, a reflection of the world we live in that still needs so much healing. Josiah explains:

> In the Afterlife, you can create anything you want. But if your motivation in earthly life was money, and you created all the wealth you wanted, you will find here that such creation is only a figment of your imagination, taken away from you after a period of time. This teaches us that there is more to life than material possessions, and also that we should not take things for granted.
>
> We find that those souls who still strive for wealth in the Afterlife are the ones who have not learned their lessons and are unwilling to grow. They have not completed their assignments or tasks, having been more concerned with their comfort and the illusion of material gain. Since they did not learn their lessons here, they will reincarnate with the same mind-set and have to repeat those lessons.
>
> It is very tempting to create an existence of great wealth in the Afterlife, but after reviewing your life in the Viewing Room and witnessing the shock of how it impacted others, you will be less likely to be led by temptation.

When I read back these messages from Josiah, I was shocked to realize how much we live in a materialistic world, and how human beings need so much more understanding and love. That may explain why people everywhere on our planet are growing so much more open to Spirit and becoming aware of spirituality. I also believe that we are generating a population of gifted children who are our future. These boys and girls are highly evolved souls who have spent longer in the Afterlife than others, so they're ready to embrace the world with the healing we all need.

It's encouraging to know that in the Afterlife, there aren't any materialistic values. When I lived in the U.K. and was giving as many as 25 readings a week, people were surprised when their departed loved ones never seemed to have much advice about finances. I've always given my clients exactly what I get, and I've rarely come across spirits who wanted to talk about problems with money, unless it was in a desperate situation. Spirits don't concern themselves with material things, so it's difficult for them to comment on this subject.

Even so, when I ask clients at the end of a session if there are any questions, most of the time they want to know if they're going to be financially secure in the future, and/or how long it will take for them to meet "Mr. [or Ms.] Right." Spirits don't tend to show me this kind of information either, because they don't have a sense of time and are not concerned about the future.

Spirits are also not judgmental. As Josiah says:

> *Souls never judge. A member of your soul family will never judge what you are doing in your life now. For example, if you decide to be in a same-sex relationship and your family members on the Earth plane disapproved, they will not judge you for your earthly choice after they pass. Life and death, as you call it, are about choices—and that is something you have to honor.*
>
> *During your time of exploration, you will stop back into the Guardianship Room to have chats with your master guide and Elder. They will decide what new tasks you need or will suggest other helpful activities for you to take on. But ultimately, what you do at this point is your choice. You can look at your progress and decide if you want to change your life, but no one can make you change. You can move forward and continue your path in*

the Afterlife, or you can decide if and when you want to return back to a new life on the Earth plane. You can go back anytime you want, and decide what it is you want to do.

∽

At this point in your healing journey, you as a soul have decided whether it is your next step to continue to stay in the Afterlife or to return to Earth and begin a new life. You may be thinking that you wouldn't want to return to the Earth plane, but the reality is that you must—unless you have fulfilled your Life Contract and are advised otherwise by the higher realms.

In the next chapter, I detail what the path is like for those staying on in the Afterlife.

∞

CHAPTER 14

HIGHER SERVICE AND MEETING GOD

At this point in your journey, you as a soul may have explored the Afterlife and decided that your lessons there were finished; therefore, you've chosen to return to the Earth plane. But know that once you return, you could very well find yourself repeating those same lessons on a deeper level. You'll also be given new lessons, as your evolution as a soul continues in earthly form, always moving toward a higher path.

However, this chapter focuses on what happens if you've chosen to stay on in the Afterlife and take the path of higher service for your evolution.

Becoming a Spirit Guide

One of the first steps on the path of service is to become a spirit guide who assists souls on the Earth plane. The level at which you enter this service, of course, will depend on your experience and whether you have been a guide before. So when you make this choice, you and your master spirit guide have many discussions about what lies ahead for you. You might learn that you're going to be his or her guide, if that soul is reincarnating. Or you may be chosen to guide some of your own soul connections, such as your soul mate or someone in your soul family.

Whom you will guide is to be determined—but not by you. The soul who is returning to Earth will make that choice, giving much consideration to who is best suited to help him or her learn the necessary lessons. It's a great honor to be asked to guide a soul, since it's an acknowledgment that you have evolved and can be trusted to take another through life's lessons.

In some cases, Life Contracts determine who guides and who is guided in any lifetime. For example, I have a contract in this lifetime with Ben, my master guide. We've swapped roles before, though—I guided him in his last life, and now he's guiding me.

If a Life Contract doesn't call for a specific arrangement, then returning souls will seek advice from their Elders about who should guide them. The Elders will then prepare the chosen guides to ensure that those souls are taken through their lives correctly and maintained on their paths.

As we know, an Elder is a highly evolved soul whose purpose is to enlighten you and help you on your journey. Your Elder is yours throughout eternity even if he or she may decide to incarnate again. You will always be connected and will never break your bond. Yet once a soul becomes evolved enough to become an Elder, that soul is usually content to stay on and help others. It's rare that he or she would see the reason to return to Earth, unless it's been requested of the Elder through a higher source.

It's important to know that Elders have all walked the Earth plane before, so they know the lessons that humans have to learn, as well as the trials and tribulations experienced in this dimension. They have lived many lives, in fact, some harder than others. They've experienced everything you can imagine—including poverty, wealth, abuse, greed, love, illness, and many other negative situations. They've gone through all of these challenges so that they truly know how to help souls preparing to become human.

People on Earth often question why their lives are so difficult, but rarely do they consider that their hardships may be there for a reason. I've been guilty of this myself on many occasions, and I've finally come to believe that we human beings have difficult lives because we're all being groomed for a higher purpose. (The fact that even Elders have experienced tough times especially proves my point.) Challenges always contain lessons that we must learn, and it's up to us to embrace those lessons—even though at the time we don't understand them. Know that whatever your particular hardship is, it's in your life to teach you something.

In the Afterlife, souls look back and review the life they've led, examining what they learned, sometimes in the midst of great hardships and challenges. They also look forward to their next incarnation and map it out fully, deciding on the events and lessons they will encounter to fulfill their contracts. When we're reborn on the Earth plane, we forget that we're always choosing to learn and grow in life, rather than to be comfortable or have an easy time.

A Period of Training

When you choose to become a guide, your regular meetings with your Elder become very important. You spend many hours (in earthly terms) with this advanced soul, who will help you develop and prepare for your role—whether that role is as an assistant on a team of guides, or a master guide overseeing the entire team. You'll be taken to lots of places and shown the wonders of existence and the universe, including several visits to the Earth plane to evaluate different lessons that the soul you guide will go through. Back in the Afterlife, you'll be taken to the Hall of Records where the Akashic Records are stored, giving you access to many of the mysteries of life to use in helping another soul through his or her incarnation.

At some point you'll be assigned to a soul who is returning to Earth. Then your training involves staying close to that soul as an opportunity to build up trust, love, and support for each other. The two of you already have a relationship as part of the same soul family, but now you must be by each other's side continuously to prepare for meeting the lessons coming in earthly life.

During this time, you will also look at the benefits of developing yourself for this role. For example, in your last life you may have had a gift of healing and helped others through their illnesses while working on your skills. Now, as one soul guiding another, you might be helping that soul develop his or her healing abilities, and in the process, strengthening your own skills even further.

Training to be a master spirit guide is quite advanced, so it's imperative that you are fully committed to taking on this position. From what Ben has told me, you must first be an assistant guide a few times before you're ready to be a master guide. In addition, you need to have some experience helping souls go through their Afterlife journey, and have accomplished much during your own time on the Earth plane.

When you prepare to be a master guide, you'll be asked to offer occasional assistance to an existing team of guides who are supporting someone through a particular challenge in life. But when you *become* one of these guides yourself, you must eventually gather your own team around you, just as you do in an earthly career when you work your way up to a higher position.

If you have mastered certain lessons and have already helped guide a soul through life, then you are eligible to be a master guide under the instruction and help of your Elder. This could be happening for you in your life right now . . . the journey you're on in this lifetime just might be leading you to become a master guide.

Being this type of guide is a huge commitment to the soul who is about to incarnate, and should only be taken on if you don't plan to go back to Earth yourself during this person's lifetime. You'll be required to stay close to the Earth plane to assist him or her, so you must be willing to step away from the joys and adventures in the Afterlife, along with your soul connections, for a while. While the majority of your time will be spent working with your assigned soul, you'll also be checking into various classrooms for extended learning, as well as connecting with your Elder. By this point, you will have built up a strong relationship with your Elder—often connecting without directly communicating, but picking up on what each other is thinking and feeling.

You'll also have a support team of guides, which will consist of souls you know and trust to help you and your charge through the many tough lessons ahead. Your team needs to be able to deal with a variety of human experiences—such as sorrow, grief, fun, laughter, becoming a parent, and many more important situations in life. However, it's up to you to make the decisions that are not only right for the soul you're guiding, but for yourself and the other guides on your team as well. Team members can step in and take over your role temporarily, but you'll always be on hand. You've been given the responsibility of managing this team, and it's one you take very seriously.

The soul you're guiding is always your first priority, which is why souls tend to take the role of master guide for their soul mates, wanting only what's best for them. However, if you're not the soul mate of the one you're guiding, there's no need to worry. You'll always have that soul's best interest at heart, as it is your duty to take care of him or her in the best possible way.

My Master Guide

Now I'd like to take a moment to tell you about my own personal master spirit guide, Ben.

As I mentioned earlier in the book, I was introduced to Ben during a visit to my grandmother. After a period of adjustment, I was able to figure out when he was near and when he wasn't—today, I recognize his presence by the tone of the words he gives me, which is always slightly lower than my own.

Ben has been around me all my life, but I have only known about him now for about nine years. However, he completely disappeared about seven years ago. Or so I thought. What happened was that he had stepped back and allowed another guide to work with me. When this new guide came in during a reading, I wasn't yet attuned to its vibrational level, and I couldn't tell who was there, if anyone! I honestly thought Ben had deserted me.

Over a period of about six months, I couldn't feel Ben at all . . . and then I was in the bathroom of a loud nightclub in London when he suddenly appeared to me once again. Naturally, I was thrilled to see him, but did he have to stand right in front of me as I was sitting on the toilet? I mean, come on—he could have found a more appropriate moment to make himself known! But no, that's Ben. It seems that our level of intimacy allows him into my most private moments.

I quickly got over any embarrassment and was greatly relieved to have my master guide back. When I was meditating a few days later, I asked him why he'd left me. He told me that he hadn't—he'd simply taken a backseat to his team for a while so he could go off and learn about the next stage I was moving into. He further explained that he'd allowed another guide to work with me so that I could get used to a different energy. That was Lucinda, who helped me while Ben was gone. I now have a good relationship with her; however, I'm still more finely attuned to Ben's energy than I am to hers.

Even though I'm referring to Ben and Lucinda as "him" and "her," souls have no gender, as I've mentioned before. But for us humans, it seems more natural to use gender when referring to our guides, only because that's what we're used to. Respecting this, guides come through to us with gender-related names that we're more comfortable with, but in their essence, they're neither male nor female. Having said that, Ben does appear as a male to me. Lucinda, on the other hand, seems female because her energy—the feeling I get when I tune in to her—is more feminine.

Whenever I work with souls who are connecting to their loved ones on the Earth plane, I'm always more highly attuned to masculine energy. That's not to say I'm unable to receive the feminine energy, which I do, but I do find this interesting.

The Kingdom of Power

In your training to be a spirit guide, you'll be taken by your Elder to places in the Afterlife you've never dreamed of before, particularly since they're so "off the map" that they're inaccessible to most. One of these is the Kingdom of Power, a remote location where the highest order of celestial beings resides, and where few are allowed to visit.

In the Kingdom of Power, your Elder takes you to meet the Source, or the Highest Master. In many earthly religions, the Highest Master is called "God," so for the sake of ease, I'll also use that term when referring to this level of celestial being.

Over the years, I've heard of such a place in the Afterlife from several souls who came through during readings. They all reported having seen a place off in the distance that glowed and radiated with warmth and love. In fact, each of them provided the same description that Josiah the Elder shares now:

There is a place in the Afterlife where only the Elders are allowed, and then only by special invitation. It is called the Kingdom of Power, and it is where the Highest Master resides, Whom some refer to as God.

The Kingdom is always visible in the distance, surrounded by rainbows and connected by a golden bridge that spans a great distance. There, the celestial beings live—the angels and all those who accompany the Almighty, whom you call God. But souls cannot just walk up to this place and knock on the door. Many try but never make it. Imagine walking and walking but never getting to your destination. No matter how far you go, your destination is always the same distance away . . . it is as if you are on a treadmill and never get anywhere!

The Kingdom is a place of exquisite peace and harmony, and a meeting with God is an enlightening and beautiful experience. There is a hierarchy in the Kingdom, but it is not driven by ego. God Himself is a higher force that governs all higher senses—such as nature, beauty, the planets, healing, comfort, and people and their growth. God governs everything, but He cannot control everything, so He sends helpers to oversee the many domains of existence. He passes on many tasks to the Elders, who pass them on to the spirit guides, who then pass them on to the living.

You can see how we are all trying to achieve God's purpose! It is about teamwork and working together. No religion, no fighting, no hassles to divide souls . . . and He wants everyone to live in harmony.

As you might imagine, it is a difficult job that God has at the moment. But things are going to change for the better, and then there will be more of a semblance of peace in the world. This may take centuries to unfold, but eventually it will come to pass.

Ben has also told me about meeting God (a rare exception, because usually only Elders do so), saying, *Imagine a meeting that is so powerful, it resonates with your soul on a deeper level than anything you have already experienced in the Afterlife.*

I've heard from spirits during readings that many souls on the other side attempt to meet God, but few actually do. Once a soul came through who'd been a priest in his last lifetime, and he surprised his sister by telling her that he hadn't met God in the Afterlife. He said that he'd seen the Kingdom of Power off in the distance and tried to reach it, but he couldn't. He was told that he was not highly evolved enough as a soul to receive an invitation, but that he should come back later when he was. He told his sister that in spite of this rebuff, he knew that God existed and loved him, but he'd have to wait some time for an invitation to actually meet Him. At that point in the reading, the soul started to laugh, coming through to say that he was still waiting for his invitation!

◌

Many of us on Earth have been aware of the presence of angels, those celestial beings who work closely with spirit guides to help us on our path. Angels are not souls who have walked the Earth plane; therefore, they don't know what it's like to go through human challenges and struggles. Yet angels will respond to our call when we need them, often taking the form of what we refer to as "guardian angels." Guardian angels will protect and guide us as our master guides do, working alongside our team of spirit guides while showing us signs to establish their presence around us.

Angels are assigned to all of us, but we have to *ask* them to work with us, which we can do anytime in our earthly lives. Every angel has a different purpose and role to play, and depending upon what our needs might be—for example *strength* or *love*—a particular angel will visit and help us. But we have to keep in mind that angels will only work for our highest good, so we can't expect them to show up with winning lottery numbers!

I remember a time in my early days as a medium when I didn't believe in angels, and I thought that people who did were a little crazy. But then I had an experience that changed me, which happened as I sat with a client one afternoon.

As the woman and I were talking, her departed husband, Jim, came through. Jim told his wife that he was with the angels, and that they were all looking after her. He promised to give her a sign that this was true, and asked her to look for it soon. Toward the end of the reading, a solitary white feather floated down from above, right before our very eyes. At the exact same moment, we both blurted out, "Jim!" in astonishment. It was the sign he said he'd send, which would confirm that he was with the angels and they were watching over my client!

Even so, my skeptical mind couldn't help but work overtime, as I looked around to see what could possibly have caused a single fluffy feather to come out of nowhere and float in front of us. There were no windows open. There were no cushions that contained feathers. There was nothing in the room to create such a thing. Bizarre!

It was then that I started to believe in angels, and I haven't doubted their existence since. Indeed, I now see them frequently, especially when I give readings to large audiences. Standing onstage in a theater, I often look up to see a huge angel suspended above the room, hovering over the space and filling it with light and warmth. Then I know I'm being protected as I connect with spirits, and that everyone I work with is imbued with love.

Yes, the celestial realms are real, as is the higher being we call Source or God. We're all being protected, guided, and loved by God, no matter what religion we follow (or don't follow). His embrace holds us all, and we're surrounded by knowledge and resources that are always abundantly available.

∽

As you can see, there is an incredible adventure awaiting you in the Afterlife—one of healing and service ruled over by a higher power who governs the entire universe. And while you're there, your Elders and guides ensure that you're always working toward your highest potential, achieving levels of mastery that further evolve you as a soul.

You're now ready to return for another cycle of earthly life and lessons. It is your turn to choose a master guide and a team of spirit guides who have been fully prepared to support you, something you do with the help of your Elder. Final arrangements await you in the Screening Room, your last stop in the Afterlife before waking up as a tiny baby in a new body on planet Earth. All of this is waiting for you in Part IV!

PART IV
RETURN

CHAPTER 15

WELCOME TO THE WORLD—AGAIN!

Although there is some information I haven't been privy to, I've tried to give you as a complete picture of the healing journey through the Afterlife as I could.

Now I want to explain what happens when souls decide to return to the Earth plane, and what the process is for their re-incarnation. This chapter will also answer any questions you might have about why returning souls choose lives that often have so many challenges and hardships along the way.

Planning Your Next Life

When you decide to return to Earth, you choose the best team of spirit guides for you, which will lead you along the path of the life you're about to enter. You discuss your decision with your soul connections, and they're all content. They know that it's part of your growth as a soul to go through another round of adventures and lessons. Some soul connections will be sad to see you leave, but they still support your decision; while others (and this could include your soul mate) know that they will in fact be joining you on the Earth plane very soon.

Once you've selected your guides, you'll be engaged in the preparation process for a while, since there is much for them to learn about what is ahead. You have been looking back on your previous life and have explored many enriching areas of the Afterlife to gather information, which you'll use as you outline the life you want to live next. Your Elder will help you with your plans, and you may find yourself visiting the Healing Rooms more frequently to deal with any issues you don't want to carry into your upcoming incarnation. This is important, as you don't want old patterns to be repeated in the new life (if you can help it).

As your new team of spirit guides helps you get ready to return to Earth, you come to know each and every one of them very intimately. You've become acquainted with many of them already, of course, but now you'll see them in a different light because they have a job or role to fulfill. The new relationship is similar to having a friend of yours become your boss—now you have two different ways of interacting with each other, one that is work related, and one that is more casual. When you incarnate, your guides will become more like your bosses, supervising your actions from a perspective you as a human won't have.

It's now time to say good-bye to your soul connections in the Afterlife. When you meet them again on the Earth plane, they will have a familiarity about them but won't be recognizable at first. You'll have experiences in which you'll look at someone and feel as if you know him or her from somewhere. It may take you a while, but eventually you'll come to recognize that you and that person are soul connected and have been together before.

Leaving the other side can be sad, but not in the same way you would grieve a loss as a human. You know that the time you're about to spend on Earth is going to be quick in relation to time in the Afterlife. Also, you know that those who are staying on can check in on you to make sure that all is going well whenever they choose.

The Screening Room

To begin your formal incarnation process, your Elder and your newly appointed master guide escort you into an area called the Screening Room, in order to make you aware of the important details of your journey.

Josiah has this to say about what goes on here:

> *The Screening Room is where you will be able to see different people who are ready to be parents, whether they realize it or not. Then you will decide where you need to be placed to best learn your lessons.*
>
> *You watch them in the Screening Room for a while, understanding which ones are the perfect match, both for you to reach your goals and for them to achieve their lessons in life. It is then that you will decide on who, as parents, will best facilitate your entry into the Earth plane.*

This is an exhilarating time for you, as you're now about to embark on a journey of lessons and challenges, but with a fresh understanding of life. Think of how exciting it is to begin a new job, when you're eager to get started and see how it all pans out. In your upcoming life, however, the lessons you'll be facing are those you'll have discussed and agreed upon with your team, so the path is already laid out to be optimal for everything you intend to accomplish.

In the Screening Room, you draw up a Life Contract with the help of your master guide and team. As Josiah explains:

> *You will be given a checklist full of lessons and goals to accomplish in the lifetime you are now entering. These items are chosen by your guides and your Elder, with your agreement, and are based on your level of evolution as a soul. You will also have a "wish list" of additional goals you want to accomplish, including experiences and events that you intend to have. Both of these lists are part of your Life Contract, but they are very different—the first being more mandatory, and the other reflecting more personal wishes and desires.*
>
> *As you map your life, you will decide which items on these lists will be most important to you. All souls must go through compiling a Life Contract before reincarnating, even troubled souls.*

In this last statement, Josiah is saying that all souls on the other side—even those who went to another healing dimension because of the harm they caused in their earthly life—must have their Life Contracts ready before they return. In these contracts are the lessons they want to learn and the people they're going to associate with; in other words, everything that's supposed to happen in their new incarnations.

We like to call the playing out of these events "fate," but the reality is we've planned them all ourselves. Therefore, when particular events happen or we meet certain individuals, we know, on some level, that it was already determined.

In the Screening Room, you preview future moments that will be particularly life changing—a divorce, a marriage, a graduation from school—which is why, in our human form, those moments occur as a vague but intriguing memory, known as déjà vu. Events shown to you in the Screening Room are absorbed by your subconscious mind and then, when that same event occurs in life, your subconscious mind says to you, *Oh, I know how that goes!* The memory is bumped into your conscious mind, giving you a sense of having "been there" before.

Choosing Your Parents

You choose your mother and father before your new body is conceived, so you're able to preview your prospective parents and their lives in the Screening Room. You can see in advance if they are the right match and will be able to give you everything you need to fulfill those items in your Life Contract that are important to you. You'll also look at their contracts and see if their goals work with yours, thus making them the right fit for you.

The parents to whom you're about to be born will give you every possible circumstance to start off learning your lessons in life, even when that means you are to be adopted or raised by other people. Remember that as souls, your mother and father have their own lessons to learn.

Josiah further explains how some souls come to be adopted:

When souls are about to be born, they have already pre-viewed the journeys that their chosen parents are on. The souls cannot control the parents' lives, but they can have some influence on their own journeys by choosing their parents. Souls already know if, at some point, one or the other parent will leave, pass, or give away his or her child; so they choose what is best for the lessons they must learn.

With information you get as a soul in the Screening Room, you match up with the parents you want. Here you plan and determine your next life . . . although when you incarnate, you probably will not not consciously recall that you have actually plotted out the course of your earthly lifetime.

All souls who want to incarnate must go through this process of choosing their parents, ensuring that they're placed with the perfect ones to help everyone learn.

In some cases, you might be returning to Earth to help your mother and father with their own lessons—in other words, it may be less about you and more about fulfilling a contract you have with another. You could be coming back to help your parents through a difficult time. Or perhaps you will leave early, which will impact them greatly. This is especially the case if you were a couple's newborn or young child, and their lessons came from dealing with your early passing.

It's important to point out here that when you return to earthly life, you don't actually enter into a body until you're ready to be born into the world. As Josiah states:

You will be with your chosen parents continuously, during the time before the conception of your new body until the birth, and then you will be with them as their newborn baby. But at any time before birth, you can decide that you are not ready to incarnate and request that the pregnancy be terminated. The Elders can also advise you on this matter, considering your own evolution, as well as that of the two people about to be your parents—who may not be right together as a couple. This is why human beings experience stillbirths and miscarriages.

In the case of a naturally terminated pregnancy or a stillbirth at full term, it's often believed that the soul has rejected the parents, causing much pain for the expectant mother and father. This is not true. Instead, such an event occurs because they as parents weren't ready for the soul or had other issues that needed to be taken care of first. The soul may then go on to be born to someone else with whom it has a soul connection, or will wait until the right time to return to its originally chosen parents.

If you as a soul decide that you came back too early because you still have more lessons to learn in the Afterlife, you can change course and reincarnate again to the same parents or at least to one of the parents who conceived your body the last time.

Sometimes a chosen parent is not willing to bring a child into the world because he or she doesn't have the right partner for it. If so, that person will stop the soul from returning as their child. Josiah sheds light on what is going on when this happens:

> *Even though you have decided that you are ready to incarnate, your chosen parents have the right to stop your entry into the world as their child. A mother or a father—or both—can change their mind about being a parent, hence the choice of abortion.*
>
> *But this choice is not a problem, since you as a soul can always return at another time, possibly to a relative close to your chosen mother and father or to another family. Or you may choose one of your parents and wait until he or she meets the right person, and come back then. It could be that your mother or father finds a new mate who wants to begin a family, or even that both parents you originally chose decide together that they are ready to have a child at a later date.*
>
> *It is all very normal for these circumstances to happen. Everyone is different in his or her choices, and among souls there is no judgment involved.*

Once you have chosen your parents, you spend the rest of your time in the Screening Room, observing them and making absolutely sure that they're the right choice for you. You're able to see everything from a few weeks before the conception to the birth. You witness the reactions of the people around your mother and father and how they're feeling. You see the pregnancy through both of your parents' eyes, understanding how they each feel about the pregnancy and about your eventual birth.

A Soul's-Eye View

As a mother myself, I know the doubts that can rock a couple when they first become pregnant, especially if their relationship isn't stable. Because of my own circumstances, I felt extremely guilty about bringing a child into an uncertain situation. However, I was assured by Spirit that the soul of my son, Charlie, would never judge me. That's because returning souls are very pure, and judgment isn't something they're likely to do.

As a soul, Charlie was observing his father, Simon, and me for some time before his birth—the truth of which I learned directly from my son himself.

Just a few weeks before Charlie was conceived, Simon and I went to Scotland for a little vacation. Neither of us had been to the area before, and we had a great time. We'd made reservations at a hotel in advance; when we arrived, however, it turned out to be overbooked, so we were moved to a hotel down the road. While there, I went shopping and bought some clothes that I didn't try on. When I got back to our room, I discovered that what I'd bought didn't fit and I'd have to take everything back. Simon and I also went to see a movie; later, at dinner, I ate salmon for the first time.

One day when Charlie was about three years old, he insisted out of the blue that he'd been to Scotland. He went on to say that he'd gone to the movies and shopping with Simon and me, that I'd gone back to the store to return some clothes, and even that I was reluctant at dinner to try salmon. I was shocked! He then told me that at first his daddy wasn't happy, since we weren't able to stay at the hotel we'd booked.

Charlie's story completely blew me away . . . especially since at the time of the events he described, he wasn't even a twinkle in my eye. There was no explanation for why he would know so many details about our trip to Scotland—after all, he hadn't been conceived yet!—other than his soul had chosen Simon and me as his parents and had been watching us the whole time.

Life's Challenges

As you can see, as a soul you know a great deal about the parents you're being born to. You also know what will happen in the life you have with them, since it's all been mapped out and planned by you beforehand. In this way, the circumstances you find yourself in will help you grow and—if you deal with them correctly—make you a stronger soul.

Life is not easy, but it's not supposed to be. Everyone must encounter challenges, as this has been the design of existence from the very beginning. Yet you may find your own challenges to be quite difficult and complain that your life is harder than most. If you find yourself looking at certain people and thinking they have it easy, know that you couldn't be more wrong. Like you, they also have lessons to learn, and their world is not as wonderful as you might imagine. What you're seeing is how they've decided to portray their lives . . . not the actuality of it.

Take celebrity couples, for example. In the glossy magazines, the rich and famous all look so happy, and their marriages and kids seem so perfect. But in reality, they have the same problems that you and I do. They're only human—they have to make career decisions, they have relationship troubles, and they might even have serious health issues. Even the most perfect-appearing marriage isn't so perfect (which I know from personal experience).

You just can't get around it: there is no perfect life. *Everyone* has difficult obstacles to overcome, and what they are exactly—

the details and the players and the circumstances—are all decided upon while souls are still in the Afterlife, long before they return to the Earth plane.

You may find that you've reincarnated to learn what you need to know for your next job in the Afterlife, such as being another soul's guide when he or she returns. Or you could be carrying out your training period by spending a lifetime in a particular family or situation. As a human, you might not understand this bigger picture; but as a soul, you know the reasons why you go through certain issues and even trauma in your life.

For example, I recall this one reading I did for a woman whose guide told me that she was going to be put in extreme danger. I relayed the guide's message, telling the woman that there would be some kind of physical abuse involved, but in the long run, she'd be okay. Her guide didn't tell me any more details, and I was thankful for that, as I didn't want to be responsible for holding back any facts.

Tragically, the woman was raped. When I saw her again, she told me that even though she'd been through a horrific ordeal, she was glad her guide hadn't warned her specifically about it. The rape had had a huge impact on her, but not in the way you might think—as a result, she'd come to realize what she wanted to do with her life. She had been aimless and unfocused in her career for years, but was now working for a rape-crisis center run by the local police in her town. She has the joy of helping other women who have had similar experiences change their lives. This woman had to go through a tragedy to make a massive change in her own life and to finally do the work she was placed on the Earth plane to do.

Coming into Your Body

Back in the Screening Room, once you've selected your future parents, you build up a lot of love and respect for them. You watch the happy times and the sad times surrounding the pregnancy, hear the music they play and stories they read to the unborn baby, and discover the names they're considering.

Parents often notice how a baby still in the womb reacts with a little kick when a certain name they're considering is mentioned or when a piece of music is played or sung. That's because even though the soul isn't in the body yet, it can influence how that body responds as it's growing to term before birth.

Finally, it's time for you to enter your new body and undergo the birth process. Josiah describes what happens now:

> *Once you are fully prepared for your return, and your body is growing in your chosen mother's womb, there will be a narrow period of time for you to enter into it. This is normally just before the time of birth, maybe a few days. When this happens, you at first experience slipping through a doorway, about to go into a free fall—but then a lifeline is instantly attached, which is your silver cord.*
>
> *You will have grown much in love for your parents over the time your body was developing, heard their every word, and felt their joy and other emotions. You will have experienced everything your mother was going through, as normally it is the mother you follow the closest. During her pregnancy, you may have witnessed an event or felt an emotion that will connect you to one person in life more than another.*
>
> *Then when the day arrives, and the first pains of childbirth hit, it will seem to you in your new body that you are under attack. During the birth process, you must be very determined to come back, and take care to protect your new body to ensure that it arrives safely for your new life.*

The journey back to the Earth plane is often traumatic for the soul. When I went through a regression-therapy session to experience my past lives, I dreaded reliving my own birth, because I'd heard it was very difficult. Thankfully, I didn't have to! But I did see visions of it during mediations, and I also experienced my soul reentering my body after having my near-death experience (NDE). The reentry happened very quickly and felt as if I were being sucked through the tube of a vacuum cleaner. Then I was hurtling rapidly down a dark tunnel and into my body. It was a strange and frightening sensation!

Josiah confirms my experience, as well as what you might recall from your own experience of returning after an NDE or from reliving your own birth:

> *Your journey back happens very quickly. You have become energetically attached to your parents through the silver cord, the lifeline that ties you to your earthly existence. You begin to feel more and more human.*
>
> *Then, when it is time to enter the physical body, often at a time when it is asleep, you experience being pulled through the brilliant White Light, flung through a long tunnel, and snapped forcibly back into physical form—a human once again.*

From my brief time in the Afterlife during my NDE, I recall how my soul felt immensely free. I knew that this wasn't going to last very long, but I was still able to feel and understand it completely. Coming into the body was a very different sensation, though. I felt crushed tight, as if my soul were trapped and being forced tightly into a body that, due to the pain of my illness, I didn't want to be in. As I landed fully in my body, a jolt of energy hit me, but not in a freeing way. It was dull and heavy, like I was supposed to feel it but couldn't. I realized later that this was because my body was protecting me, preventing what would have been a very painful experience at the time.

Josiah further describes the process that exactly parallels what I went through, and may be familiar to you as well:

> *The rebirth process is hard for you, since it is painful in both body and soul. Many souls do not want to go through it, but others cannot wait to get it over with. It begins when you see a tunnel, and upon entering it, you lose your sense of freedom and feel extremely restricted. You push your way through the long, dark corridor—unused to being so squeezed and confined—and eventually, you see a light. This is the light of the human world.*

The hands that grab you and pull you into this world are strange, but when you are placed into the arms of a person who seems familiar, a surge of love fills your every cell. You will feel instantly at home and comforted by this person, as you have known and loved her for so long, not only in the world that you have come from, but probably in so many other lives you have lived on Earth before.

~

Once again, you're welcomed back to your earthly home, to embark upon the great adventure of learning and growth. As a soul you have survived, passed from life to Afterlife, from Afterlife to life again, and so on through your evolution. What you encounter in your time on Earth, you will see again after you have passed, so make the best of it—there is no escaping your own evolution!

CHAPTER 16

LIVING IN THE NOW

As I was writing this book and attempting to shed light on the survival of the soul, I naturally questioned some of the information I'd been given. This was my own skeptical mind at work, just as yours may have been as you read these pages.

Personally, I always think it's good to be somewhat skeptical, particularly since human beings are conditioned to be this way. However, I've had to step out of that skeptical box and trust, which is why I meditated periodically during the writing process, making sure that I was receiving information in the very best way I could.

I have always told the people who come to me to learn psychic ability and mediumship that they must trust their own instincts and gut reactions, just as my Nan Frances taught me to do all those years ago.

So even though I may have been skeptical at first, I love what I have received and channeled! It's apparent to me that the guides and other souls who helped me through this journey have presented the information in a way that the human mind can accept and relate to. For this, I am very blessed.

As I look back on the survival of the soul, I see that the process is complex and incredible—but most of all, it's beautiful. The Afterlife is filled with love and comfort beyond anything we can comprehend on the Earth plane. But with the knowledge we now have of the other side, I believe that we're hugely helped to live the best life we can in the present, *right now*.

Being in this moment and living "in the now" is truly what is most important. We can't always look at our life and be thinking *What if?* We have to accept *what is* and what has happened, and then we must move forward, one step at a time.

If someone close to you has passed on, know that he or she is with you and watching over you, ensuring that you are well. It will help you to know now that this person's life was mapped out to go exactly as it did—there are no mistakes. We are all where we're supposed to be right in this very moment, and that is also true for souls who are now in the Afterlife.

Here I'd like to assure you that your beloved animals and pets go through the same process when they pass that humans do. As souls, they will be there for you when you pass, waiting in the Afterlife. But that's a whole other book entirely!

It's your choice to live with an expanded mind and the spiritual knowledge that you are an eternal soul. How you progress down the pathway of life is entirely up to you, because you do have free will. Just remember that whatever you go through is preparing you for the next stage of your journey, whatever that may be.

So now when you go through the good and the bad times, know that there is a reason for it all. You can embrace everything with love and a smile, for eventually it will all work out in the way that it's supposed to. Remember that you planned the life you have for a reason. You orchestrated certain people to come into your life for a purpose—that of teaching you lessons and making you grow.

There is a higher purpose for *all* of this. And yes, you have to come back to do it all over again, but it's a voyage of self-discovery and a powerful adventure!

It is the survival of the soul. . . .

Epilogue

After I finished writing this book, a remarkable event occurred that sheds further light on the journey we'll all take to the Afterlife.

There is a reason I served as a channel for my dear friend Elaine, whom I helped during her transition. Although the emotion of her passing is still raw for me, I want to share the experience with you. My hope is that you will be informed and inspired by this story, and seek to connect with your own departed loved one. You see, even though communicating with Spirit is a gift, the signs that are sent can appear to anyone who is open to messages from a soul who has passed and with whom they share a loving bond.

I asked Elaine's daughter Jennie if I could tell our story to the readers of *The Survival of the Soul,* and she felt honored that I would do so. She believes, as do I, that her mother's passing will help others realize that beyond a doubt, the soul survives.

∽

Elaine Saller was a mother figure, a confidante, and a shoulder to cry on—even though she'd have me laughing before I knew it. Most of all, she was the dearest and most wonderful friend I could ever have. On the surface our relationship may not have seemed to make much sense, because she was almost 30 years older than I am. But age was irrelevant for us, as our connection was not physical but truly one of the soul.

I never expected somebody to walk into my life and impact it in the way she did. Just by being who she was, Elaine gave me the inspiration and courage to know that I could do anything I put my mind to. She continues to do this, even in her passing.

Elaine was from Philly and had a feisty way about her. No one could stand in her way—and if you crossed someone she cared about, God help you. She never let anything in life get her down, not even when the going got tough.

She was also a talker, and she used to drive me crazy with the stories I'd already heard about 50 times. She always had to make noise whenever there was silence, and even talked in her sleep. I smile affectionately when I think of it, because that was just her—always a tale to tell, as well as a laugh you couldn't help but join. She was, quite simply, one hell of a wonderful woman.

My dear friend blossomed in the last two years she was on the planet, enjoying life to the fullest. Her social life would have put Paris Hilton's to shame. Yet although she had a vast amount of friends, nothing got in the way of her family, especially her two beautiful daughters and their children. She also had the most amazing relationship with her ex-husband, whom she still considered family. I was blessed to be part of that family, too, having been fully accepted into the Saller fold.

During Thanksgiving week in 2008, Elaine and I joined another friend of hers, Marilyn, at Arizona's famous Canyon Ranch spa. We happily relaxed, took fitness classes, and let ourselves be pampered. Nothing stopped Elaine: she exercised vigorously every chance she got; spoiled herself silly; and even flirted with the younger men who helped out at the spa, joking that she wasn't a cougar, but a saber-toothed tiger!

She only complained once during our stay, and it was of a slight pain in her hip. I was off duty, not in my psychic medium ("witchy woo") mode, so I didn't think anything of it. I did tell her to get her hip checked out, but that was it. The two of us focused on having fun and enjoying the week with each other and Marilyn.

Almost a year later, as I was leaving Australia to return to the States, I got an e-mail from Elaine. She never e-mailed, preferring to pick up the phone and chat, so I was very surprised. She wrote that she had to have a biopsy for a lump that had come up in her neck, but she didn't feel it was anything serious. I didn't want to think that it could be serious either, so I never switched to my witchy-woo mode to look deeper. But I now realize that I was being protective of myself, not wanting to know the truth about my friend.

I landed back in the U.S. and immediately turned on my cell phone to find a message from Elaine. She said it turned out that she had cancer, but then added in her own inimitable way, "I'm going to fight the fucker!" *Oh, that's so Elaine!* I thought. Before I'd even left the plane, I called her and said, "Okay, that just means you have to suffer me twice a week for healing, doesn't it?" and we both laughed.

For the next five months, when I wasn't traveling, I went to see her. I'd drop Charlie off at school on Tuesdays and Fridays and then head straight to Elaine's home. In many ways, it was my escape from the world, as nothing interfered with our time together. We'd ignore our calls and other interruptions . . . and it was bliss. She even remained silent as I shared healing energy with her through my ability as a Reiki practitioner. I think I was the only one who could get her to be quiet—and I did!—at least until I felt the healing energy going into her body. Then as soon as she felt that infusion, she'd suddenly be off again, talking about everything under the sun!

To look at Elaine, you would never have guessed that she had cancer. And she remained positive about her illness, going to work most days and still enjoying her active social life, even though her chemotherapy schedule was grueling. Of course, even then she was so full of spirit and fun that everyone wanted to have chemo with her—it became a social event for her and those she shared it with.

The holiday season came along, and I was out shopping for gifts when I came across two beautiful champagne glasses with Swarovski crystals embedded in the stem. They were stunning, and since they screamed *Elaine!* I bought them.

The next time I went to see my friend, she said, "Oh my God, Lisa, I have found *the* most amazing gift for you for Christmas. You are just going to love it! But I can't go and get it because I can't risk being in the stores with so many people having colds or the flu." I totally understood, of course. And anyway, I already had the best gift—I had Elaine.

She never could keep a secret, though, so as I was leaving to get my gift for her from the car, she blurted out, "You are going to die when you see what I want to get you for Christmas. They're Swarovski-crystal champagne glasses!"

After telling her to hold that thought, I went out to my car and returned with a box. After she'd unwrapped it, I said, "These aren't the glasses, are they?" Neither of us could get over how connected we were, to the point that we'd planned on getting each other the same gift! She insisted that I keep the glasses I gave her, and then when she got hers, we'd swap.

✑

One morning in February, I'd just come back to my office from a healing session with Elaine when my friend Jonesy asked me how Elaine was doing. I burst into tears. There was no logical reason for my response, because she'd been told by her doctor that she was heading into remission. Even so, I told Jonesy that I didn't think Elaine was going to survive.

That night I went home, got the two crystal glasses out of their box, and put them on the top shelf of my glass cabinet for a special occasion. I never told Elaine that she wouldn't survive; in fact, every time she asked me if she was going to be okay, I always told her yes, meaning that her *soul* would be fine. In my consciousness, I wanted to believe that she'd beat the cancer—but in my soul, I knew otherwise. I chose to believe my consciousness.

From February on, I could see the change in my friend. Even though she remained positive, it was as though she knew something. Now there were periods of quiet between us in the healing sessions, which was so unlike her. One time she was telling me about a situation in her life that was preoccupying her mind, when I asked, "You've given up, haven't you?" She said yes. Both of us may have thought that we were talking about her situation, but on a soul level, we were talking about her cancer.

I think I was the only one who knew how she truly felt. She may have been facing reality in her soul, but her consciousness didn't want to and kept fighting. She even spoke of a remission party she'd planned, and said that she and I should go back to Canyon Ranch to celebrate around my birthday in June. She was adamant that she'd be disease free by then.

Yet I slowly saw her fight become weaker and weaker, as though she was accepting the inevitable. She even spoke of getting home help to come stay with her, as she knew things were going to get bad. I never thought I'd hear these words come out of her mouth. My friend had fought for so many other things in her life, and those around her thought that she was fighting her illness the same way. But she started to confide in me about making a will and the like, to ensure that her girls were taken care of. She was clearly looking to put her house in order.

On a Monday in April, I'd just returned from a trip to Hawaii when I found out that Elaine had been in the hospital for the past week with a blood clot. When I told her that I was on my way for a healing session, I was surprised to hear her say she was resting. I knew something more was up than that she didn't want me to see her without makeup and in her pj's—both of which I'd seen plenty of times over the years.

I didn't let on, of course, but that's when I started the grieving process for her. I cried so hard that I didn't know what to do. All I could think of was to call a friend of hers and ask him to meet me at her house in the morning, so I wouldn't be the only one who got shouted at. Yes, I was actually scared of this—even though Elaine was weak, she still had that feisty side to her and would hate for me to turn up unannounced and see her in her current condition.

I arrived at Elaine's on Tuesday morning and was greeted by the home help. I was told that her friend was already with her in her bedroom, and I went in to see that Elaine was very sleepy and in a great deal of pain. I came close and told her that I'd put my hands on her for healing while she rested.

"I don't know where my crystals are," she replied. We always worked with crystals in our healing sessions, and trust her to think of that! I told her not to worry about it and placed my hands on her. At that moment my worst fears were confirmed, and I had to face facts—this was it. I gently allowed the healing energy to go into her body, and her body took what it needed. I was careful not to overwhelm her, and while she was conscious I made her promise to see her doctor.

All of a sudden, she said, "There's a reason why we met." We'd both always thought that we'd come together because we were going through marriage separations at the same time. Yet the truth was that I'd come into her life to help her soul, and she'd came into mine to give me the courage I needed to do anything I put my mind to.

Elaine went into the hospital that night, and I went to see her the next morning and promised to be back the following day. That Thursday, I arrived at the hospital around 3 P.M.—and when she looked at me, I could see her soul. It was the same thing that had happened with my granddad, and I didn't like it. Elaine's daughter told me that the doctor had explained to her and her sister that unless their mother found the strength to fight this, he couldn't give her the chemo that she needed, and she wouldn't survive.

I placed my hands on Elaine until an attorney friend of hers arrived. They spoke for a while, and she kept thanking him for everything he'd done that day. It was as if she knew that this was the last day she'd be coherent and able to deal with such matters.

Then it was just the two of us in the room. She grabbed my hand, sat up, and looked me directly in the eye. "Something is going on—why are all these people here?" she asked, referring to the friends who'd come to visit her. "I know that you know."

I didn't think she needed to know what the doctor had said, because she had to keep fighting no matter what. So I just told her that I wasn't sure what was going on.

But then she looked at me soul to soul, and asked, "Am I going to survive the night, Lisa?" She was so serious and intent on knowing the answer that I couldn't lie to her. "Honestly, Elaine, I don't know," I replied. How I wish I could have given her a different answer, but I really *didn't* know.

At that point she requested that I not leave her, and that I help her through whatever was ahead. I felt honored to be asked to be there for one of the most private and intimate moments that would ever happen to her.

Elaine then called one of her daughters in and started to speak to her about legal matters, but she didn't want to hear it. I insisted that her daughter listen, however, because of the many readings I've done where people regretted that they hadn't paid better attention to their loved one's last words.

I stayed at the hospital until midnight. When I left, I insisted the girls call me at the slightest change so I could come right back.

The next morning I woke up at 6:55 because I heard Elaine call my name. Five minutes later, I was up, brushing my teeth, getting dressed, and trying to text her daughter all at the same time, when a message came through: *Please come.*

I rushed downstairs to find Charlie and Inma, my assistant, both busy building a LEGO construction. I gave a quick kiss good-bye to my son and told him I'd see him after school, so thankful that Inma could look after him.

I was at the hospital 15 minutes later. The girls were shocked that I'd gotten there so quickly, and I joked that I drive a sports car for a reason—it sure comes in handy sometimes. But the truth was that since I'd been woken up by Elaine's soul, I knew I needed to get to the hospital ASAP.

My friend had deteriorated throughout the night but still had some fight left in her. She struggled to breathe, but I was right there with healing energy to calm her. Her body was accepting the healing that it needed, and on a soul level she knew it was going to help her. She would wake up, look right at people, smile, and say that she was "fucking fighting" this thing, so everyone still had a glimmer of hope. But she couldn't look at me—if we *had* looked at each other, she would have seen the truth and so would I. It was very difficult for me to accept and deal with this. However, I had to remain strong and positive to support her loved ones, and to give her what she needed when she needed it.

It was on this day that the family left her bedside to arrange the funeral service, which according to the Jewish religion had to happen only a few days after her passing. Again, I stayed until midnight and then returned early the next morning. At around 8 A.M. on Saturday, we decided to do some furniture rearranging so that we could get everyone in who'd be visiting, moving Elaine into the middle of the room.

She remained every bit herself, swearing at the girls, telling them to be quiet because she needed peace and quiet to fight this "fucking thing." You couldn't help but laugh—her body may have been getting weaker by the day, but her spirit was still so strong and fierce, and she was fighting with everything she had.

Even so, that day was the hardest one. I started the morning holding on to her legs and giving her healing energy. I could feel her soul trying to leave her body, but then a thought would come in and she'd come back with a thud. No one else seemed to experience this except me.

At one point people in the room were sobbing softly, thinking that Elaine was sleeping. I felt her soul briefly leave her body to converse with the spirits who had come to collect her and had congregated behind her bed. Then I heard, *Tell them all to stop fucking crying!* (I'm sure you've gathered by now that she liked to use the F word!)

I could tell that Elaine's soul needed to leave her body so that she could prepare for her crossing and be out of pain. Yet although I was called upon many times to help her breathe, there wasn't much else I could do at that point.

A close friend of hers who was also a rabbi came to visit, and she started to mumble. Suddenly, clear as a bell, she said, "He's a fucking schmuck!"

"I hope you're not talking to me, Elaine," he said, and we all laughed. (We're still not sure who she was talking about.)

The rabbi stayed, and we all prayed together, which was a very intimate and special experience. About an hour after he left, I was back to giving her some healing energy. She started to talk, and we all leaned forward to hear her. She addressed the girls, telling them to stay true to themselves and be happy, and to look after each other and their children. Then she told everyone in the room that we were all special to her, each in our own way. She asked for the family to make a circle of love around her. Each daughter held one of her hands, and I put my hand on top of one hand and my other on her head. We all took turns telling her what we were thankful for and how she'd impacted our lives.

Later, she and I were the only ones in the room. She told me she had to pee and tried to get up and walk to the bathroom. When I stopped her, she said, "You're right, Lisa. I should stay here. But I'm scared." I told her not to be, that I'd be there to see her soul over and that she had to trust me. I assured her again that I wouldn't leave her. And I didn't.

I stayed overnight, sleeping with my head resting on a pillow at her feet. I kept one eye open, though, and listened to her breathing to make sure she wasn't struggling. Every time she woke up, I was there with energy and helped her stay calm. That's really all I could do at that point: be a calming influence as she went through the inevitable.

Sunday came, and it was the day everyone had been dreading, since Elaine's daughters had a very difficult decision to make. They decided that her morphine should be increased to the highest level, so she'd be out of pain. We all had a moment on our own with her and told her we loved her. She was still there and trying to talk to her daughters, but fluid was restricting her throat, so I was the only one who could understand her.

I know now that I was hearing her on a soul level, but my consciousness was kicking in, too. It was very strange. She often said that she was afraid, which is something I chose not to share with the others. Instead, I conversed with her on a soul-to-soul level, telling her it was time to let go and that everyone was going to be okay.

Later we found out that back at Elaine's house, where all the grandchildren were staying, the lights began flickering that evening. And Charlie was getting restless at our home—Inma told me that he asked her if he could sleep in my bed at 9:35 P.M., which was when I felt Elaine's transition begin.

At that moment Elaine's daughter Jennie felt her mother coming to her as the room grew cold. I could see the spirits closing in around my friend, and I opened my arms to help her receive them. I felt her alight in my open arms, her soul very heavy from the battle. Her soul stayed resting in my arms for what seemed like five minutes, but in reality was only a few seconds. I heard *Tell everyone I love them*, and then her soul left my arms. She needed to be at peace.

People said their good-byes to her and began to leave, even though Elaine was still breathing. I'd come so far that I didn't want to leave, but I also didn't want to intrude on the last moments her daughters had with her.

Around 12:30 A.M. on Monday, April 26, 2010, I was about to leave when Jennie stopped me to thank me for all I'd done. Suddenly, I felt this burst of energy and heard these words: *Oh no you don't!*

Devrha, Elaine's other daughter, was sleeping by her mother's side and holding her hand when I came back in the room and started to time Elaine's breathing.

"Dev, wake up," Jennie and I said together, realizing that the end was near. All three of us were there to see Elaine take her last breath.

It was a peaceful, calm, and easy passing; but I believe Elaine had some influence in how it went. She'd sent out the message: *Oh no, you can't leave me until the very last minute—and if you're not going to stay, I'm going now!* Later, we all laughed about her persistent spirit.

Elaine's passing was the most intimate, bittersweet moment I've ever experienced. Although I'd already written this book and become familiar with the process, I knew I needed to share the experience of her passing because it would help so many people. I'd lost a friend whom I loved very deeply, but I'd also been there to witness her final moments, which were beautiful and reassuring. And to have held her soul in my arms . . . there are no words to describe how incredible that felt.

◦⁄◦

Charlie had overheard a conversation I'd had with Inma, so he knew I'd been at the hospital with Elaine. He repeatedly told me, "Mommy, I don't want you to come home until Elaine is better." And I did exactly that.

On the night of her passing, I sat at home and told my son what had really happened. Elaine *was* better now, I assured him—her soul was at peace, freed from a tired body that was no longer of any use to her.

I decided that it was time to dust off the glasses I'd bought for Elaine. Charlie took one, a tiny bit of champagne in the bottom, and I took the other. The two of us lifted the crystal flutes and toasted that fantastic lady, laughing and sharing our favorite memories of her.

The following weekend, Elaine's daughter Devrha stopped by for a visit. I got the glasses out again, and in honor of her mom, we drank more some bubbly. I finished mine and washed the glass, placing it carefully in the middle of the drying mat so that it wouldn't break.

We were talking when Dev suddenly shouted, "No!" I turned around in time to watch the crystal glass slowly fall. The stem broke as the base of the glass hit the kitchen counter, and all the crystals scattered. It was as if Elaine were saying, *Oh no . . . we drink out of those glasses!* and left me with only one of them. Since then, I've decided to have a piece of jewelry made with those crystals in it, which I can wear in memory of Elaine.

Another sign happened on May 26, exactly a month to the day after Elaine passed away. Charlie and I found 26 dead wasps in the house, lying next to her photo. Scouring the outside area for a nest, we found nothing—and we never saw another wasp, dead or alive. Later we found Elaine's picture on the floor with a crystal from the glass by the side of it. This was strange, since the photo was in the family room and the glass had broken in the kitchen.

There have been so many signs to show me that Elaine's soul is still connected to us all, but the most special one was given the night before her funeral, when she came to me to give me personal messages for the special people in her life that she wanted me to deliver the next day. Before the funeral, I inscribed each message on cards she'd chosen through me at a store that morning, and then I gave them out. It was a beautiful gesture and assured us all that Elaine's spirit was watching over us, full of love and as strong as ever!

Even though I have communicated with Spirit for many years, Elaine's passing has given me a deeper insight into the power that we have within our soul. I feel very blessed to have had the experience of being with her as she passed, as sad as it may have been, and I know that sharing it here will help many people on their own pathway through life and death. Elaine may not be physically around, but she is still helping, guiding and inspiring me to talk about *the survival of the soul.*

❧

ACKNOWLEDGMENTS

There are many people who have influenced my life throughout the writing of this book, and I am very grateful to each and every one of them. I wish to extend special thanks to:

Charlie, for being the special soul you are, and for making sure I smile every day, even when times were tough.

Holly, for making me see the light and helping me to believe in myself. You are an incredible inspiration, and I am so blessed and grateful to have you as part of my life. I love you.

Jonesy and Caroline, thank you for making sure that I stayed on track and completed deadlines. I know it wasn't an easy task!

Mike, for inspiring me and giving me guidance in how to write a book . . . you are a star!

Janey, thanks for being there and allowing me to cry on your shoulder and vent. You have kept me on track in so many ways through this tough journey; you are my soul sister and always will be. Love you, chick!

Michelle and Sarah, thank you for reading and believing in my work. You have questioned it and helped me write in a way that everyone is able to understand. Thank you so much!

Ryan, Steve, and Double D; thanks for taking care of me on the road and always making me laugh. Now I'll be able to hang and be fun and not constantly say, "I have a book to write!"

Mark, my manager and friend, you have always been there to support and guide me. Thank you!

Reid Tracy, Louise Hay, and the rest of the Hay House team; thank you for believing in my gift and giving me the platform on which I can stand to help and teach others about the survival of the soul.

Nancy Marriott, my editor, I couldn't have done this without your hard work, love, and passion for this book. You have been a blessing in my life, and I hope that this is just the start of a harmonious relationship.

To my LW Members and those who have supported my gift, thank you. I cannot express how much it means to me to know that you're behind me, and I thank you for the words of encouragement and love. You really are within my heart!

There are so many others who need to be thanked, but you know who you are. Know that you are always in my heart, and I thank the universe for putting you in my life.

∞

ABOUT THE AUTHOR

Lisa Williams is known and loved around the world as a medium and clairvoyant with an amazing ability to communicate with those who have passed on to the other side. Born in England, Lisa was discovered by Merv Griffin and introduced to audiences through two seasons of her own hit show, *Lisa Williams: Life Among the Dead;* along with *Lisa Williams: Voices from the Other Side* and *Lisa Williams Live.* All series are now airing around the world.

Lisa is the author of *Life Among the Dead;* and has appeared on *Oprah, Good Morning America, Larry King Live,* and *Jimmy Kimmel Live.* She is currently on tour performing in front of large live audiences worldwide, and blogs regularly about her life and spiritual teachings at: **www.lisawilliams.com**, where she interacts with the public as well as her site members.

Lisa is also a trained Reiki and crystal healer. She lives in Southern California with her son, Charlie; and their two dogs, Lucy and Max.

NOTES

NOTES

NOTES

NOTES

We hope you enjoyed this Hay House book. If you'd like to receive our online catalog featuring additional information on Hay House books and products, or if you'd like to find out more about the Hay Foundation, please contact:

Hay House, Inc., P.O. Box 5100, Carlsbad, CA 92018-5100
(760) 431-7695 or (800) 654-5126
(760) 431-6948 (fax) or (800) 650-5115 (fax)
www.hayhouse.com® • **www.hayfoundation.org**

❧

Published and distributed in Australia by: Hay House Australia Pty. Ltd., 18/36 Ralph St., Alexandria NSW 2015 • *Phone:* 612-9669-4299 *Fax:* 612-9669-4144 • www.hayhouse.com.au

Published and distributed in the United Kingdom by: Hay House UK, Ltd., 292B Kensal Rd., London W10 5BE • *Phone:* 44-20-8962-1230 *Fax:* 44-20-8962-1239 • www.hayhouse.co.uk

Published and distributed in the Republic of South Africa by: Hay House SA (Pty), Ltd., P.O. Box 990, Witkoppen 2068 • *Phone/Fax:* 27-11-467-8904 www.hayhouse.co.za

Published in India by: Hay House Publishers India, Muskaan Complex, Plot No. 3, B-2, Vasant Kunj, New Delhi 110 070 • *Phone:* 91-11-4176-1620 *Fax:* 91-11-4176-1630 • www.hayhouse.co.in

Distributed in Canada by: Raincoast, 9050 Shaughnessy St., Vancouver, B.C. V6P 6E5 • *Phone:* (604) 323-7100 • *Fax:* (604) 323-2600 • www.raincoast.com

❧

Take Your Soul on a Vacation

Visit **www.HealYourLife.com®** to regroup, recharge, and reconnect with your own magnificence. Featuring blogs, mind-body-spirit news, and life-changing wisdom from Louise Hay and friends.

Visit **www.HealYourLife.com** today!